In June 1955 West Germany was the scene of NATO atomic war games in which, according to official estimates, 1,700,000 were "killed" and 3,500,000 "wounded." The name given to these war games was OPERATION CARTE BLANCHE.

Our modern generals have sometimes been likened to Homer's heroes who would make long speeches before starting to fight. I feel it would be more appropriate to compare them to the god Pan. His appearance caused panic and, through his fear-inspiring voice, he was able to rout the Titans who had risen against the gods.

Let us not forget, however, that one day, while the gods held a banquet on the banks of the Nile, Typhon suddenly appeared and Pan fled, awe-stricken. He plunged into the river where he remained immersed to the waist. Thereupon he was transformed into CAPRICORN, goat from the waist up and fish from the waist down, and Zeus placed the monster in the sky to commemorate what had happened.

May the peoples of the world lift their eyes to the stars and learn a useful lesson before giving *carte blanche.* . . .

Let them take care not to follow the lead of the animal of which it is said in the Russian proverb: "The pig spends its life with its snout in the dung heap. It sees the sky for the first time at the moment when it gets butchered."

EDOUARD LE GHAIT

No Carte Blanche to Capricorn

to Capricorn

THE FOLLY OF NUCLEAR WAR STRATEGY

EDOUARD LE GHAIT

Former Ambassador
and Chef de Cabinet, Belgian Foreign Ministry

BOOKFIELD HOUSE

NEW YORK

Contents

		Page
	Introduction	7
I.	Capricorn	9
II.	Tight-Rope Walking, Brinkmanship and Procrastination	12
III.	Defense, Deterrence and Provocation	25
IV.	Limitation and "Escalation"	55
V.	"Hugging Technique" and Disengagement	73
VI.	Bucks and Bangs	82
VII.	Penguins and Seals	87

Introduction

This little book reproduces with a few changes and additions a study I had written in French and printed for private circulation in Belgium at the beginning of this year. My purpose at the time was to acquaint a few people in my country with some of the ideas on modern strategy expounded in the United States and in Great Britain. Literature in French on the subject is comparatively scarce. People on the continent of Europe are on the whole very ignorant of the problems connected with their chances of survival and even persons in responsible quarters are sometimes surprisingly misinformed.

My conviction is that the present tendency of NATO strategy to rely on the confined territory of overpopulated Western Europe as a base for more and more powerful nuclear weapons rests on a most precarious basis, namely ignorance of matters of modern strategy in the countries concerned.

If this be so, the situation is fraught with great political danger. Unless war breaks out soon, in which case Western Europe would be completely obliterated, people will gradually become aware of the tremendous risks entailed by NATO strategy and the arrival of IRBM missiles in great numbers. A growing hostility may well develop among European nations towards governments that sponsor the Atlantic alliance and even towards the United States itself.

Recent disturbances in Japan comprise a lesson it would be unwise to ignore. Reasons for opposition to the presence of strategic bases are fundamentally the same in Europe and in Japan. But Europeans, not having experienced Hiroshima and Nagasaki, are less alert to the danger than the Japanese.

As Bertrand Russell put it recently in a letter to the London *New Statesman* of July 9, 1960, present policy "makes it not improbable that the whole population of Britain may be exterminated without bringing on a world war." Very few minds are as keen as that of Lord Russell but, given time, the essential facts

7

are likely to be grasped even by the dullest, and such comprehension might prove fatal to the Atlantic alliance.

I believe there is an urgent need for the Western World to rethink its whole policy; it must devise a strategy which entails risks for its members which, if they are not exactly equal, are at least of the same order of magnitude. I believe this can be done without jeopardizing the West's deterrent power, while it would at the same time greatly reduce the probability of war.

The existence in the United States of an abundant and very remarkable literature on modern strategy precludes me from thinking I am able to present American readers with anything very new on the subject. I am myself greatly indebted to the admirable and penetrating analyses made by American authors and particularly by certain members of the Rand Corporation. My comments may, however, serve a useful purpose if they draw the attention of some Americans to the dangers of an inter-Allied strategy based, not on a conscious and enlightened approval by the peoples concerned, but rather on the ambitions of a few leaders (these few are apt to become many and that is not the least disquieting aspect of the problem) aiming to reach with American aid a position where they will be fully able to play the old game of power politics.

Close friendship and cooperation between the peoples of Western Europe and North America are essential if humanity is to survive in some orderly fashion the present period of extraordinarily rapid evolution and if the civilized values which we cherish equally on both sides of the Atlantic are to be preserved. For this reason strategy must not be determined by the ambitions of the very few or the short-term interests of a small minority, but must be subordinated to the need for strengthening the Atlantic alliance in the mind of the common man by giving him and his children the best chances of survival in this dangerous world we live in.

May these comments of mine stimulate the reader to think of ways and means to achieve this goal.

August 8, 1960   Edward Le Ghait

I
Capricorn

I N JUNE 1955 WEST GERMANY WAS THE SCENE OF NATO WAR
games in which the Air Force, by making use of tactical
atomic weapons, was to fight an invasion presumed to have
come from the East. Three hundred thirty-five atomic projectiles
with an explosive power of between two and 40 kilotons of TNT
were supposedly launched. According to official estimates
1,700,000 Germans would have been killed and 3,500,000
wounded in such an operation. These figures are considered by
highly responsible commentators as fictions calculated to give
the public the idea that tactical atomic weapons are in no way
more deadly than conventional weapons.

As a matter of fact war games also took place that same
year in Louisiana, with 275 atomic projectiles of the same
capacity presumably dropped over an area larger than that
used for the German maneuvers; and the "referees" interpreted
the results to mean that "all life had ceased to exist" in
Louisiana.

Regardless of interpretation, however, the German ex-
periment brought home to some Europeans the meaning of
"limited" nuclear war, restricted to tactical atomic weapons—the
dream of many military men.

During the last few decades the general staffs, and sometimes civilian agencies as well, have made it a practice to desig-
nate by a code name the actual or simulated operations in which
they are engaged. Quite often this term is symptomatic of both
the nature of the operation and the mentality of its authors.

Thus the assassination of King Alexander of Yugoslavia
and Mr. Barthou was termed "Operation Teutonic Sword," the

landing in Normandy in 1944 was coded "Operation Overload" and the explosion of the big thermonuclear bomb at Bikini on March 1, 1954 was designated "Operation Shot Bravo." Sometimes there is a kind of tragic irony in these terms, as when the United States Atomic Energy Commission labeled the worldwide study of radioactive fallout caused by nuclear explosions "Project Sunshine."

"Operation Carte Blanche" was the name for the NATO war games of June 1955 already referred to. Speculation on the psychological reasons underlying this epithet is wide open. In any event this term is a good illustration of the kind of power which the recent fantastic advances in the development of means of destruction have placed in the hands of those controlling them.

In no other field has technical progress made such terrifying strides as in the field of destructive devices. A corollary of this advance has been the increasing importance of military men in our society. Many people have expressed misgivings on this state of affairs, since wielding the sword is not exactly the best training for control of the atom. Moreover, the fact that the military men of certain countries are increasingly losing the habit of silence which once characterized their status in the civilized world has aroused criticism. The sometimes ill-timed remarks made by military leaders have created doubts in the public mind as to the wisdom and level-headedness of the men in whose hands modern technology has placed the fate of nations. Many have come to look back wistfully to the days of the "great and silent soldier."

It should be pointed out in this connection that the intrusion of the military into the realm of the word is by no means accidental, but rather a logical consequence of the nature of modern armaments.

Even the most fervent advocates of nuclear arms concede, unless of course they have lost their sense of proportion, that these weapons can guarantee national defense—the purpose for which they were intended—only so long as they remain unused. According to this concept, peace can be guaranteed by nuclear weapons provided the potential opponents are fully convinced that firing these weapons would mean general suicide.

In the past, national defense used to be guaranteed by the very existence of weapons as well as by the fear these inspired. Nuclear weapons, on the other hand, can be useful to national defense solely through the fear they engender. In the atomic age, having the potential adversary know and fully understand the devastating nature of the weapons in one's own arsenal (and one's unswerving intention to make use of them if necessary) has become a *sine qua non* of their usefulness.

Under these circumstances it is understandable that military leaders, promoted from being mere arms bearers, should have become policymakers too. With the concept of peace predicated on the balance of terror, they are exceptionally qualified to boast of their arms and intimidate the opponent. Formerly propaganda was an accessory in the organization of national defense. Today it constitutes its most vital part. Usefulness in the art of handling and controlling weapons is today predicated on the mastery of the spoken and written word.

Our modern generals have sometimes been likened to Homer's heroes who would make long speeches before starting to fight. I feel it would be more appropriate to compare them to the god Pan. His appearance caused panic and, through his fear-inspiring voice, he was able to rout the Titans who had risen against the gods.

Let us not forget, however, that one day, while the gods held a banquet on the banks of the Nile, Typhon suddenly appeared and Pan fled, awe-stricken. He plunged into the river where he remained immersed to the waist. Thereupon he was transformed into Capricorn, goat from the waist up and fish from the waist down, and Zeus placed the monster in the sky to commemorate what had happened.

May the peoples of the world lift their eyes to the stars and learn a useful lesson before giving *carte blanche.* . . .

Let them take care not to follow the lead of that animal of which it is said in the Russian proverb: "The pig spends its life with its snout in the dung heap. It sees the sky for the first time at the moment when it gets butchered."

11

II

Tight-Rope Walking, Brinkmanship and Procrastination

IT IS NOT ACCIDENTAL THAT THE MILITARY MEN OF NATO SHOULD have termed their great war games "Operation Carte Blanche." In the January 1959 issue of the periodical *Aussenpolitik,* published in Stuttgart, General Frido von Senger und Etterlin proves that there are in fact no political checks within NATO on strategic decisions, that NATO has no political entity competent to act in the matter. The general states in particular: "To maintain that the NATO Council itself guarantees the primacy of policy-making in decisions on military matters would be misleading. The Council is not in a position to do anything of that kind." And further on, he writes, "The preponderance of military bureaucracy under Allied Command is without any precedent in history."

Although the question of peace and war is of much greater importance in the atomic era than in the time of Clemenceau, it now rests, to a point never before permitted in countries with democratic governments, in the hands of military men.

We witness a sort of abdication of political power before technology, of the civilian agency before the military. In the face of the complexity of the problem and the heavy burden of responsibility, politicians are tempted to hide behind the advice of their technical consultants. Most of the time political parties try as best they can to ignore the problems raised by the existence of nuclear weapons and prefer to address their constituents on matters whose importance is paltry by comparison. If in exceptional cases a political party gives the question of the danger of atomic warfare the attention it deserves, the voters show no appreciation at all. The defeat of the Labor Party in the last British elections is a case in point. To a party that squarely faced up to the question of the H-bomb the voters preferred one which had never seriously concerned itself with this all-important problem.

We must admit that the apparent indifference of political parties toward atomic danger is only a reflection of the general attitude. The public prefers to hear about bread, prosperity and pleasant times ahead rather than about those terrifying dangers whose scope surpasses all understanding and against which it feels powerless. This attitude has deep psychological causes. In a remarkable article in the *Atlantic Monthly* of November 1958 Dr. J. D. Frank, Professor of Psychiatry at Johns Hopkins Medical School, draws a parallel between the attitudes of people facing the atomic danger and that of many mental patients. Both tend to reject the notion that danger is threatening them. Both are suffering from what Freud termed "repetition compulsion" which forces them to repeat the very actions that are the cause of their illness. As the patient's anguish increases his behavior pattern becomes more set. The more threatening the arms race, the greater the tendency to accelerate it.

The tendency to deny the existence of danger, carried to the extreme in the mentally ill, is in fact a basic human trait. Life would be difficult to bear without it. Courage, a virtue so related to the negation of danger, is one of the qualities that have made the survival of our species possible. As Shakespeare made Julius Caesar say so aptly:

> Cowards die many times before their deaths;
> The valiant never taste of death but once.

When danger originates in external causes beyond the control of man, the denial of its existence offers many advantages

13

from the psychological point of view, often without harmful consequences. But when the danger is man-made and may be eliminated by man, then the tendency to deny that it exists becomes serious indeed, for it prevents him from generating the will for remedial action.

In the course of the millennia of evolution mankind has developed the reflexes necessary for survival. Truly a weak reed dependent on the forces of nature, man developed reflexes permitting him to adapt to those changing external influences over which he had no control. But these same reflexes cannot protect him against self-made danger. More serious still, they may even have an action-inhibiting effect and may paralyze him in the face of the terrible consequences of his growing knowledge.

In the past survival was essentially a problem of adapting to environment. Today it has become mainly a problem of controlling the changes brought about in his environment by man himself.

Making public opinion aware of this new situation in which mankind has been placed by the discovery of nuclear energy constitutes one of the most urgent tasks for today. Yet continuous pressure from the masses is indispensable. Otherwise those who, whether by chance, ambition or personal merit, are heads of nations, cannot, even if their intentions are good, ward off the tragic fate seemingly in store for us.

It is dangerous for public opinion to accommodate itself to peace predicated on a balance of terror and to let itself be lulled into believing in its stability. For this balance is essentially unstable, based as it is on such unpredictable assumptions as the mental equilibrium of each of the individuals in a position to upset it. Furthermore the number of these individuals on both sides is likely to grow in proportion as technical progress requires more and more acceptance of strategic concepts in which the speed of possible retaliation becomes increasingly important.

Two years ago General Omar Bradley stated:

> We are speeding inexorably toward a day when even the ingenuity of our scientists may be unable to save us from the

consequences of a single rash act or a lone reckless hand upon the switch of an uninterceptible missile.

The passive attitude, let alone the indifference of the majority in the face of the atomic peril, tends to give *carte blanche* to certain civilian and military personnel. We like to think of them as "competent," although their intellectual make-up is hardly conducive to their understanding of the new situation.

The belief is widespread that the very enormity of the disaster which war would cause is today a guarantee against its outbreak. This optimistic view takes for granted that reason will always prevail among the leaders of great countries. It disregards the fact that ambition, whether personal or national, has a tendency to precipitate gambling and sometimes blindness in the face of impending danger.

In an article in *Le Monde* of November 7, 1959 we see even as astute a person as General Billotte succumbing to this dangerous optimism. He begins by stating very aptly:

> Each one of the opponents now possesses the means to destroy his adversary several times over. What good is it to be twice, three, four or n-times more powerful than one's opponent if the latter must in any event be constantly ready to retaliate with total destruction? In addition it is also necessary to protect oneself against such retaliation. However, although a reliable anti-aircraft defense based on ground-to-air missiles was still quite conceivable in the age of bombers, even supersonic ones, it has become problematical, not to say illusory, against bombers that can launch air-to-ground missiles from great distances; and all the more so where ground-to-ground missiles are concerned.

But then he declares:

> Huge sums are therefore being spent every year for the preparation of a war which, we can say as a fair guess, will never occur . . . unless the folly of man should push us to collective suicide, which after all is hardly plausible. Never before would rivals have wasted such huge sums merely to reach a stalemate. The dreadful aspect of the arms race is only equaled by its futility; the only other result it may produce is to hamper or arrest completely economic and social progress.

We are unable to share General Billotte's optimism. If the arms race continues, chances are that it will constitute a good deal more than a simple waste of resources and that it will sooner or later lead to war and, perhaps, to the end of the world.

The folly of those in power has played an important part throughout history and General Billotte underestimates the probability of its continuing to do so in the future. Events of the recent past have proved that even in the 20th century a Caligula could very well become the head of a world power.

Indeed in any dispute with a country in possession of nuclear weapons, unless retaliatory action could be prevented, these weapons would constitute an *ultima ratio,* one which is truly *ultima,* for their application would be equivalent to suicide.

Certainly one might think it is highly unlikely in the foreseeable future for anyone deliberately to unleash a nuclear war. But great historical events are not as a rule the result of conscious human decisions. Rather, they are often the consequence of a number of circumstances created by human decisions which, at the time they are taken, appear to their originators quite innocent or else are meant to produce totally different effects.

Tolstoy analyzed this problem in *War and Peace.* It is incorrect to say that it was on the day after the Battle of Borodino that Marshal Kutuzov made his decision to evacuate Moscow. Actually the evacuation was the inevitable result of a series of prior decisions which at the time had been of secondary importance.

In history most of the time the "die is cast" long before it seems to be.

An action apparently involving few risks may very well trigger a war—and a nuclear war most easily of all.

General Billotte has failed to take into account the possible consequences of the policy of "calculated risks." Recent history unfortunately does not warrant the belief that this policy is now unfashionable.

In all calculations there is a possibility of error, and errors in judgment are especially frequent.

With the advent of the nuclear age the risks involved in such calculations became so great that a new word had to be coined properly to denote the policy of those "calculated risks" of which John Foster Dulles boasted mastery. This term is the so-called "brinkmanship."

In a book published at the beginning of 1959 and entitled *Common Sense and Nuclear Warfare,* Bertrand Russell states with regard to "brinkmanship":

> . . . This is a policy adapted from a sport which, I am told, is practiced by the sons of very rich Americans. This sport is called 'Chicken!' It is played by choosing a long straight road with a white line down the middle and starting two very fast cars toward each other from opposite ends. Each car is expected to keep the wheels of one side on the white line. As they approach each other, mutual destruction becomes more and more imminent. If one of them swerves from the white line before the other, the other as he passes shouts, 'Chicken!' and the one who has swerved becomes an object of contempt. As played by youthful plutocrats this game is considered decadent and immoral, though only the lives of the players are risked. But when the game is played by eminent statesmen who risk not only their own lives but those of many hundreds of millions of human beings, it is thought on both sides that the statesmen on one side are displaying a high degree of wisdom and courage and only the statesmen on the other side are reprehensible. This of course is absurd. Both are to blame for playing such an incredibly dangerous game. The game may be played without misfortune a few times, but sooner or later it will come to be felt that loss of face is more dreadful than nuclear annihilation. The moment will come when neither side can face the derisive cry of 'Chicken!' from the other side. When that moment is come, the statesmen of both sides will plunge the world into destruction.

A belief widely held by public opinion is that in the nuclear age the heads of state are as exposed to the perils of war as the rest of the population. This is supposed to guarantee that they will act wisely and work for the maintenance of peace.

17

We should not allow ourselves to be misled as to the importance of this attitude. The danger of under-evaluation of risks is great, especially where heads of state are inclined to ambition or to taking chances, or want to go down in history as "virtuosi of brinkmanship." Every day we can see men risking their lives in pursuits which to others may seem rather futile. Statesmen and military leaders are not necessarily more niggardly with the spilling of their own blood than, for example, the contestants in car races. And it would seem that the prospect of glory derived from a diplomatic or military victory is at least as intoxicating as that of the Grand Prix. Both involve the same tendency to act rashly.

When we study the question of how heads of state calculate risks to which they feel they can or must subject the population, we must not forget that the interests and the motives of the heads of states are never identical with those of the governed.

Again to quote Bertrand Russell:

> Whatever the purpose of an organization, its government derives satisfaction from power, and has, in consequence, an interest not identical with that of the members.

The tendency of statesmen to consider the nations they rule as tools subservient to their own ambition or vanity has existed throughout the ages. It may be found with Cheops as well as with Hitler.

All through history the concept that a government must work for its people to better their living conditions, that the State (that is to say, the statesmen themselves) must serve its citizens, has only occasionally been the guiding principle of those in power. It is for that reason that the message embodied in the Declaration of Independence of the United States of America had such repercussions around the world.

Lincoln took on as a self-appointed task "... to elevate the condition of men; to lift artificial weights from all shoulders; to clear the paths of laudable pursuit for all; to afford all an unfettered start and a fair chance in the race of life." But Lincoln was an exceptional personality and it is for this reason, and rightly so, that his name continues to be reverently remembered.

The concept of the State as an end in itself comes quite naturally to those who consider themselves synonymous with it and for whom, though in varying degree, *"l'état, c'est moi,"* as it was for Louis XIV. Sometimes an entire ideology is worked out to make this concept palatable to the masses and often "the vital and uppermost interests of the country" are nothing more than the vital and uppermost interests of individuals.

A striking example of the influence of personal factors in the assessment of risks to which certain numbers of persons are exposed is the sinking of the *Titanic*. In April 1912 this magnificent transatlantic liner, the pride of the White Star Line, which had just come out of the shipyard, made its first Atlantic crossing. The company president was on board ship. The *Titanic*, fitted out with the most modern equipment, constructed according to the latest technical developments, was to shatter all speed records for the ocean crossing and thus on its very first trip to win the famed blue ribbon. Then one evening radio messages relayed to the *Titanic* from other ships warn it of the presence of icebergs along its scheduled route. To avoid the danger the Captain wants to change course, take a more southerly lane. But according to reliable accounts the company president objects: there would be a delay and the *Titanic* would lose its chance to win the blue ribbon. Blinded to danger by his desire for glory, unable to resign himself to giving up the coveted trophy, he exerts pressure on the Captain and insists that the shortest possible route must still be followed . . . The result: catastrophe! It is doubtful if among the fifteen hundred persons who were lost there were many who would have chosen to risk their lives for the blue ribbon. Had they been consulted, they would probably have assessed the situation quite differently.

Another aspect of the risk calculation question, a highly complex one, deserves our attention here. How much bearing do the size and importance of the stake itself have on determining what constitutes an acceptable risk? It would seem that this is predicated not so much on absolute values as on the subjective response of the one making the decision. Thus the head of a nation of one hundred million would be willing to accept for his people the same degree of risk as he would if his country consisted of only one million inhabitants. On the other hand there can be no doubt that a head of state is likely to accept a greater risk for only a segment of his country than for the entire population. In other words, the head of the country of one hundred million would assume a larger risk for one million of his people than he would if that million represented his *entire* country. It follows that insofar as the security of a country's population depends on the calculation of risks made by its leaders, it is not in the people's interests to be part of a large political unity.

During the summer of 1958 the atomic submarine *Skate* came to Europe after having crossed the North Pole by navigating under the icecap. It was welcomed in the ports of several countries. The Danish Government however refused it permission to enter the port of Copenhagen, feeling quite rightly that the risk of an explosion, although very small in itself, was too great considering the proportions of a possible disaster and the great values at stake: the capital and a large section of the population of the kingdom. The Danish Government evidenced in this case keen awareness of its responsibilities and a clear understanding of the necessity for letting the possible acceptable risk depend on the value of the factors at stake. It is rather symptomatic of our times that the attitude of the Danish Government was generally misunderstood. International public opinion once again on this occasion displayed its incapacity to grasp the essential features of the problems brought about by the atomic era. In some instances it even went so far as to put on airs of condescending charity toward the physicists the Danish Government had consulted, undoubtedly forgetting that these men, and Niels Bohr in particular, had been among the first to discover the properties of the atom.

Had Copenhagen been a small provincial town in a large political entity rather than the capital of a small kingdom, chances are that government authorities would have allowed the *Skate* to enter its port. The safety of only a small segment of the population entrusted to their care would have been at stake

20

and, according to our thesis, they could have afforded to be less demanding in assessing the factors of acceptable risk.

It can easily be seen why the Prince of Monaco should decline the honor of welcoming the *Skate* into the port of Monte Carlo. It is much more difficult to imagine the French Republic refusing it entry into one of her ports of equal size.

The instance of the *Skate* visit calls for second thoughts. Contrary to an opinion all too glibly embraced, the security of individuals is not always promoted by integration into large entities.

The scatterbrains who, in the small countries, clamor in season and out for European or other integration would do well to ponder this aspect of the question.

Along with the factors which may have an unfortunate influence on calculation of risks is inurement to danger, an attitude which may have an unfavorable effect on the wisdom of governments. Inurement to danger may arise within a government as well as among the governed. When a dangerous situation continues to exist for some time without precipitating accidents, the belief is engendered that the danger has disappeared. Furthermore, danger which threatens a group is generally harder for one of its members to discern than danger threatening the individual alone. From the psychological viewpoint it is much easier to "live dangerously" within the group than outside of it. The group as such imparts an illusory sense of security.

This is a highly important phenomenon which is partly responsible for the strange behavior of humanity in this day and age. Just because the balance of terror has continued to exist for a few years without causing an accident, people now tend to believe in a stability of the situation and accommodate themselves to it. There is superficial acknowledgment of the fact that the problem of disarmament is the most important one we must tackle, yet we act as if there were no urgency about settling it.

For two years there has been talk of a Summit meeting. But some people stress the need for "minute preparation" first while others warn against any "undue haste."

The half-heartedness with which the countries of the West have answered the advances made by Mr. Khrushchev in the past few years with an insistence and an obstinacy rare in a representative of a big power reveals a disturbing lack of understanding on the part of Western leaders of the pressing need for a solution of our problems. They seem to have forgotten that if politics is the art of the possible it is also one which requires the ability to seize favorable opportunities, and that these are often elusive.

In the meantime, while "a prudent lack of haste" prevails in the chancelleries and while world leaders compete with one another in the art of procrastination, the fate of mankind teeters on a tightrope. The fact that a nuclear accident or an error of judgment could precipitate total war becomes day by day more probable. Atomic weapons multiply and the means of instantaneous retaliation are improved to the point of absolute reliability.

Each day that passes without a start having been made on dealing effectively with the disarmament question is one more day of opportunity for a possible accident.

In spite of all the precautions we take a certain number of plane and railroad accidents each year are inevitable. They are, in fact, a statistical certainty. We know from experience that in spite of all possible precautionary measures, trains cannot run indefinitely over a railroad network without producing a single accident. It is difficult to conceive that the continued stockpiling of nuclear weapons all ready to be set off at an instant's notice will *never* lead to some accident due either to human or to mechanical failure. An airplane or train accident produces only limited damage and injury. But with all the means of instantaneous retaliation now being installed, the involuntary explosion of a single bomb may trigger a hundred or thousand others, putting an end to our civilization.

As early as 1957, Dr. Pickering, Director of Research at the California Institute of Technology, wrote that in the not too distant future the decision to destroy the enemy would be made by an electronic brain unaided by human intelligence and that our lives would then become contingent on the proper functioning of a machine which, should it for example mistake meteors for missiles, might become the cause of the end of our civilization.

But these prospects do not seem to have any influence on politicians and diplomats. For them, if disarmament is the subject, there is no hurry. In August 1959 it was decided to establish a new Disarmament Commission composed of the representatives of five countries of the West and five of the East. The first meeting of this Commission took place on March 15, 1960.

Similar procrastination was one of the important causes of the Second World War. Sir Philip Noel-Baker, former British Minister and recipient of the 1959 Nobel Peace Prize, in his book, *The Arms Race,* described it as follows:

> . . . But the governments, and in particular the Governments of Britain and France, delayed too long in putting forward proposals on the basis of which a general disarmament could certainly have been made. The Geneva Disarmament Conference ultimately met in February 1932; it was not till March 1933 that the British Government laid before it a comprehensive Draft Convention which Sir Anthony Eden had prepared. There was a general consensus of opinion at the time that, if this had come at the beginning instead of at the end, the Conference could hardly have failed . . .
>
> But the British Government, like the French, took too long to make up its mind that disarming itself was better than allowing Germany to rearm; by the time it had done so, Hitler was in power and the Conference was dead.

We have tried to point out some of the factors which, even on certain vital questions, prompt political leaders to adopt attitudes that have little in common with the interests of the people they govern.

In the atomic age this tendency makes it particularly important for the governed to be in a position to control, criticize and correct the policy of their governments.

Unfortunately problems of strategic scope become more and more complex; understanding their true nature becomes more and more the exclusive domain of specialists who of necessity are working for the governments.

Thus for arriving at some sort of independent and detailed view of the important problems on which their own lives and those of their children depend, the citizenry have only incomplete information at their disposal and insufficient time for proper study. Nevertheless there is available even now a considerable amount of literature on strategy for survival in the atomic era. It is the duty of all those able to do so to familiarize themselves with the subject. Through them the masses should be given to understand the essential features of the problems they will have to solve if they want to survive.

Only greater awareness of the problem of survival on the part of a larger part of the citizenry can prevent the continuation of ominous and dangerous policies that sometimes are based on old-fashioned concepts, sometimes merely thoughtlessly adopted.

In his recent book, *Strategy for Survival,* Wayland Young, after denouncing the lies of which officialdom has been guilty, concludes:

> If we are to save ourselves, should we not be told what threatens us? It is an arrogant or a desperate government which believes it can face the greatest crisis ever to afflict conscious life on this globe with the help only of those minds which it has paid and sworn to secrecy. Let us be told everything, and let us, all over the world, consider what we have been told and allow it to permeate our minds and inform our thoughts and our feelings. Then and only then can the whole weight of human wisdom be brought to bear on slowly and painfully devising a new pattern of life which will allow us to continue.

III

Defense, Deterrence and Provocation

A CCORDING TO AN OLD SAYING, A NEW MEANS OF DEFENSE CAN always be found to check a new means of offense.

Our history bears out this statement; however the check is never absolutely foolproof and is never instantly available. The development of defensive arms follows after some delay that of offensive weapons, resulting in a new balance between them.

The advent of nuclear weapons and missiles has upset this course of action. The prodigious headstart that the discovery of nuclear energy gave the means of destruction also gave offensive weapons a formidable and perhaps irretrievable lead over defensive ones.

Right now the combination of ballistic missiles and thermonuclear bombs forms an offensive potential against which it is highly unlikely that adequate means of defense can be found.

It is not out of the question that within certain limits some means of defense against missiles may be discovered. The United States intends in the next few years to spend huge sums for just such research work. But with each of the potential opponents having sufficient means of destruction at his disposal to annihilate his enemy several times over, defense systems should be one hundred per cent efficient. Indeed the success of even a fraction of the adversary's means of offense is enough to inflict fatal injury. Under these conditions it is difficult to conceive that a really adequate defense system will be found.

In *The New Scientist* of April 2, 1959, Dr. Tom Margerison makes the following comment:

> The reason why the hydrogen bomb is such a deadly partner to the ballistic missile is that it makes much more efficient defense systems necessary. During the last war, when bombers carried conventional high explosives to drop on London, a defense system which prevented two-thirds of the raiders from reaching their target area could be considered very effective. The cost of such a raid to the enemy was high and the damage inflicted on the target relatively low. All this has been changed with the coming of nuclear weapons for a single hydrogen bomb could obliterate the greater part of London. In other words any defense system worth having nowadays must have a very good chance of destroying every hydrogen bomb before it reaches its target.

This decisive victory of offensive over defensive arms completely revolutionizes existing strategic concepts. The concept of "defense" tends to be replaced by that of "deterrence." Unfortunately, however, a policy of deterrence is generally interpreted as a policy of intimidation by those it is supposed to dissuade.

The concept of deterrence is as old as history. As the proverb says, *"Si vis pacem, para bellum."* But modern technology endows it with a completely new dimension.

The purpose of defense systems has always been, first and foremost, to deter, to dissuade opponents from venturing an attack. Only if this aim could not be achieved were they utilized as active means of defense.

There is, however, a basic difference between the deterrent role of the weapons of the pre-atomic age and of nuclear and thermonuclear weapons.

In the past, weapons utilized as deterrents were principally of a defensive nature. Naturally, an army was often used for offensive as well as for defensive purposes. Even fortifications whose main purpose was the protection of a country against invasion could on occasion serve as a shield for troop concentrations intended for offensive operations. Coastal fortifications served the dual purpose of providing shelter for corsairs and repulsing hostile maritime raids. Generally speaking, however, deterrent weapons did not constitute a direct and immediate threat to the potential enemy. Their role was rather similar to that of the thorns in the coat-of-arms of Louis XI: "He who rubs against them shall feel their sting."

Thermonuclear deterrent weapons are a different matter altogether. They have a purely offensive character. In the eyes of the potential opponent they are a terrible, total, and immediate threat. Like a sword of Damocles they hang suspended over his head, perhaps not by the proverbial hair but by that equally risky guarantee of safety, the nerves of his potential enemies.

At first sight thermonuclear bombs that may be launched by ballistic missiles seem such a radical deterrent that one would think they would make other weapons superfluous.

But in actuality the question is far more complex, since for a deterrent to play its part two essential conditions must first be fulfilled:

1) The deterrent must be capable of being "the second to fire." It must be incapable of being put out of action before retaliating. Failing to meet this condition, a deterrent would not only fail to play the role for which it was intended but would also become a temptation for the opponent, an invitation for him to attack in order to destroy it. The capacity for returning the blow, for reprisals or "retaliation," is an essential element for a deterrent of the type of the sword of Damocles.

2) The deterrent must be fully reliable. This reliability will depend upon the circumstances. It will prove considerable if its implicit threat is not counterbalanced by enemy threats of a similar magnitude. It will be that much weaker should the contrary be the case. Thus the efficiency of a deterrent is always relative.

To fulfill the first condition the deterrent must be rendered as invulnerable as possible. The opponent must feel he cannot put it out of action before it can retaliate. We shall re-examine this question later on. To satisfy the second condition, the cure should not be worse than the disease. The carrying out of the threat contained in the deterrent should not bring down on its possessor consequences far worse than those he wishes to prevent.

If one power holds a monopoly on nuclear weapons and their means of delivery, it is obviously unlikely that any other power will attack it. This, from the point of view of the possessor of nuclear weapons, is the ideal situation. In such a case the weapons' deterrent power is fully playing its part. This held true for the United States from 1945 to 1949. However, it would be unfair to blame American diplomacy of that period for not having known how to put this nuclear monopoly to better advantage. The number of atomic bombs held by the United States at that time was limited, the means for their delivery not fully dependable. On the day after the bombing of Nagasaki, at the moment of Japan's surrender, the United States no longer had a single atomic bomb.

In 1949 the first explosion of a Soviet atomic bomb put an end to this American monopoly. But during the next few years and up to about three years ago the United States continued to hold a strategic nuclear superiority and could thus exercise a deterrent power whose evolution was described in a pamphlet published by the Advisory Council of the Democratic National Committee:

> The deterrent effect which our superior nuclear forces had upon Soviet policy in this situation has been called "active deterrence." It reached beyond protecting us against direct attack and modified the conduct of the potential aggressor in other ways. It was this "active deterrence" which the Administration (Republican) was exploiting when it announced the national strategy described by the press as "massive retaliation." This laid upon the Strategic Air Command the task of defending our allies everywhere, as well as the United States, against threatened Communist attack. Even then, however, the Soviet Union, though still relatively weak in nuclear weapons and delivery means, had significant capacity for administering nuclear destruction, particularly against our allies in Western Europe, which she might have

used if pushed to the wall. This capacity on her part set limits on the use *we* could make of our "active" deterrent. Its positive utility was limited. This possession of nuclear destructive capacity limited to last-resort use if threatened with attack or after actual attack has been called "passive" deterrence.

It was our "active" deterrent power which diminished as the Soviet Union grew in nuclear strength. There was, of course, nothing unforeseeable about this, particularly after the Russians mastered the H-bomb in 1953. It explains why "massive retaliation" turned out to be such a perishable strategy. For, in the state of nuclear parity, "active deterrence" is attenuated, if not lost altogether, and powers in the state of nuclear parity retain largely "passive deterrence," deterrence against direct attack. This rests upon the aggressor's belief that a direct attack, which does not destroy his victim's power to retaliate, will bring back upon him unacceptable damage. At the same time, the "active" aspect of the deterrent weakens as the prospective user of strategic nuclear weapons contemplates the unacceptable damage to his own country which the use will surely bring upon it.

Furthermore, as we permit the Russians to achieve a lead in strategic missiles, *their* deterrent power becomes increasingly "active" while our strategic force continues to lose what "active" significance remains to it. If we permit the Russians to achieve a decisive missile superiority, so that we cannot even be sure of our ability to administer a telling second strike, not only will our strategic power be stripped of its "active" significance, but also even its ultimate value as a "passive" deterrent will be placed in jeopardy. That is why it is of first importance that we have the position of parity in strategic power. . . .

This analysis of the functioning of deterrence may be complemented by citing as an example of "active deterrence" Bulganin's intervention in the 1956 Suez crisis. Soviet deterrence, which had been passive up to that time, suddenly turned active, while France and Great Britain were deprived of United States support.

If the carrying out of the threat contained in the deterrent is likely to spell suicide for the nation holding it, the deterrent becomes inoperative under all circumstances where the nation's very existence is not at stake. Deterrents based on thermonuclear bombs cannot be utilized to influence conflicts of only secondary importance arising between great nuclear powers.

Ever since United States territory has been within range of intercontinental Soviet missiles the value of the protection guaranteed to Western Europe by the great American deterrent has become doubtful indeed, certainly where limited Soviet action might not directly threaten the United States itself. Those who are anxious to see European governments possess their own atomic weapons did not fail to make the most of this argument.

To counteract the weakness of the great deterrent held by the American Strategic Air Command, NATO has complemented it with secondary deterrents. General Norstad, in a speech given at the Atlantic Congress in London on June 6, 1959, described their purpose in the following terms:

> . . . As seen from NATO Europe, the deterrent is made up of two major elements: the heavy strategic forces, which are sometimes called the retaliatory forces, and the Shield Forces under my command. Taken as a whole, the heavy strategic forces constitute one side—the heavy side—of the deterrent. Although these forces could be used, and used effectively if need be, against lesser challenges, their full power would be needed only to meet a major challenge. It is the existence and the effectiveness of these heavy forces that must be considered by an aggressor who contemplates an act which might lead to major involvement. When considered in these terms, a deliberate decision to provoke a major war becomes most improbable—the price of aggression becomes too great.

> Thus perhaps the greatest danger might spring from a weakness inviting exploitation—from a probing operation which might well get out of hand as the result of a miscalculation. In short, from a mistake. With this in mind we have arrived at what we consider the basic objectives of any valid strategy for Europe. First, in the event of an incident, a clash, whether intentional or unintentional, we must be able to force a pause, to compel a break in the continuity of the action that has started. Second, during this pause an aggressor must be forced to make a conscious decision. He must be compelled to realize that by continuing the action he chooses war with all its consequences to him. Third, when he is considering this decision he

30

must at all times be forced to weigh the total cost of his action. He must consider the full price that may be exacted by bringing into operation the full efforts of all the forces and factors that make up the deterrent throughout the world.

The Shield Forces of NATO are designed to achieve these objectives, and thus they have an essential role within the deterrent. This vital Shield consists of ground forces, air forces and naval forces which are deployed in the forward areas and participate in the forward defenses. The Shield Forces are not limited to conventional units, equipment or operations. They do have that independent capacity, of course, but they also are armed with nuclear weapons. They are designed to accomplish their mission of preventing war, of defending Europe against a broad range of threats.

The Shield has three military functions:

One is traditional in nature: Its forces must defend the easternmost peoples and territories of the Alliance, and in so doing contribute to the defense of the entire NATO area. This defense involves holding Europe against a full range of possible attack, up to aggression in its heaviest form. The forces must be adequate in number and they must be capable of dealing with both nuclear and non-nuclear situations.

The second function is more complex. If composed, as it must be, of forces maintained in a high state of readiness and capable of meeting even an attack in substantial force, the Shield can deny to the aggressor the inviting prospect of conquering Europe piecemeal or by the sheer weight of his masses. Our forces need not be massive in comparison with those that might be thrown against them; but the Shield must be strong enough, and its resources sufficiently versatile, beyond all possible doubt, to deal decisively with any attack short of the unmistakable, deliberate, all-out aggression which would invoke the heavy side of the deterrent.

Function three springs from the one I have just mentioned. By reason of its mixed capabilities, nuclear and non-nuclear, the Shield is designed to make possible a more flexible response by our forces, and by our diplomacy, in a region where any challenge could have the gravest implications. As I have stated, a rational strategy in this nuclear era is one that offers an interval for deliberation, that compels an aggressor to make a

31

conscious decision for war. Were the Shield Forces too weak to deal with an attack against them, this requirement would not be established and the alternatives facing us would be either to accept defeat on the narrow ground of the enemy's choice, or to risk a general war. If, however, we have strength enough in our Shield Forces, the dilemma passes to the aggressor. It is the aggressor who then must weigh the power not only of the forces directly in front of him, but also of all other elements of the deterrent. It is the aggressor who then must choose between risking all or attempting nothing.

NATO strategy is thus depicted as a Shield enabling the Sword, represented by the Strategic Air Command, to intervene only as a last resort.

The explanations given by General Norstad regarding the tasks assigned to the NATO Shield are not entirely convincing. Those alleged local attacks by an enemy with inadequate armaments against which the Shield is supposed to protect us appear to be quite outside the realm of probability.

Lost patrols could be readily redirected by a simple cordon of troops. No need whatsoever would arise to use military units equipped with nuclear weapons. Moreover it is difficult to imagine the Soviets engaging in forays large enough to require the use of such nuclear weapons for repulsing such attacks without a decision from their high authorities, in full awareness of the consequences. One might conceivably imagine the Soviets launching an offensive in Europe—assuming inaction by the Strategic Air Command—but it is inconceivable that they would undertake such an offensive with forces obviously inferior to those the Shield would place against them, merely for the fun of being driven back.

If General Norstad really believes that the greatest danger lies in a state of local "weakness" likely to "tempt the opponent to take undue advantage," then the Western Governments' attitude and their determination to make no changes in the status of Berlin becomes incomprehensible. Indeed if there is one point of "weakness" likely to "invite taking advantage of," it is certainly that of the Allied troops in West Berlin. The very fact that these troops have for so many years remained relatively unmolested in so abnormal a situation, without serious incidents occurring, even before the war potential of the NATO Shield was there to protect them, proves that a state of local weakness does not prevent the continued existence of a situation based on the balance of powerful deterrents.

If General Norstad's explanations carry little conviction, it is probably not because he really believes that the Russians would act like reckless children who know not what they do, but rather because the Supreme Allied Commander in Europe can ill afford publicly to cast doubt on the reliability of the powerful American deterrent and thus force the real problem out into the open.

Indeed General Norstad must know better than anybody else that the Russians would never undertake an offensive in Europe unless they were ready for a clash with the Strategic Air Command or else could take the latter's inaction fully for granted.

The actual purpose of NATO's Shield is, by forcing the Russians to supply powerful means for any projected offensive against Western Europe, to heighten the reliability of the great deterrent. The arsenal of nuclear weapons of the NATO units precludes any possibility of an offensive to be undertaken with conventional weapons alone. Even were it conceivable that by some miracle hostilities conducted with conventional weapons in so vital a theater of operations as Europe would not *ipso facto* set off the great deterrents, it would be still more impossible to imagine that, conversely, the thermonuclear explosion of these deterrents would not promptly follow those of atomic bombs detonated over the NATO Shield.

We do not feel that such an obviously problematic and doubtless superfluous increase in deterrent effect justifies the enormous risks involved in providing the armies facing each other in Central Europe with nuclear weapons.

Chances are that any incident arising in the future would only have wider repercussions if these armies are so equipped. In the case of atomic hostilities breaking out in Europe the panic everywhere would immediately become such that the great deterrents, in order to be the first to fire, would go off of their own accord.

The nuclear armaments of the NATO Shield and the correlative armaments of the Soviet Armed Forces provide the mechanism which guarantees the almost automatic outbreak of thermonuclear war. No individual, no government would have to assume clear-cut responsibility. In this way nobody would be forced to face the painful dilemmas suggested by General Norstad. The events themselves would have provided the catastrophe in its full scope. The obstacles that the scruples of human conscience might place in the way of strategic considerations would thus be bypassed.

What happens to our sense of responsibility when it is faced with situations created by the existence of modern weapons is effectively illustrated by General Norstad's postulation that we must try to leave it up to the opponent to make the decision on which the ultimate fate of the human race will depend.

We already pointed out that in order for a deterrent to fulfill its role it must be rendered as invulnerable as possible. The potential of the newest offensive weapons has made national defense impossible, at least in the sense in which this term was used in the pre-atomic era. National defense has been replaced by the deterrent and by defense of the deterrent.

Public opinion in most countries does not yet realize that in the domain of nuclear strategy the only technically attainable goal in matters of national defense is defense of the deterrent itself. Defense of the nation, of its citizens, of its cities and its countryside is an impossibility!

This is a fact which can no longer be argued and which has been given official recognition.

As far back as August 1957—when ballistic missiles had not yet reached the stage of development they have today and when planes equipped with thermonuclear bombs were still the most dangerous existing offensive weapons—Mr. Duncan Sandys, then Minister of Defense of Great Britain, admitted that should war occur, it would be impossible to prevent a certain

34

number of H-bomb carrying planes from reaching Great Britain. He added, "That is why we have taken a very bold decision in deciding not to do the impossible. We decided not to defend the whole country, but to defend only our bomber bases."

Thus national defense is restricted to protecting one's ability to carry out reprisals against the enemy. What was true in 1957 is truer still today and will be even more so tomorrow, when bombers, which are highly vulnerable, will have been replaced by ballistic missiles and with planes equipped with air-to-ground missiles.

Unwillingly perhaps, by admitting a "boldness not to attempt the impossible," Mr. Duncan Sandys clearly revealed the power of the forces that tend to make nations and governments follow the beaten path. With the advent of the nuclear era this can only lead to positions from which there is no return.

How and to what extent can a deterrent be made invulnerable? Total invulnerability is impossible to achieve, for nothing can resist a direct H-bomb hit. But the invulnerability of a deterrent can be considered proportionate to the number of H-bombs required to destroy it.

Leaving aside the complementary and secondary deterrent effect of "tactical" nuclear forces (equipped with atomic bombs with an explosive power measured in kilotons of TNT), we may consider that the deterrent is essentially made up of thermonuclear bombs (with an explosive force measured in megatons of TNT) and of their means of delivery. These are planes with a wide radius of action or long-range ballistic missiles, since the bases for both, whether airfields or rocket launching platforms, must, in order not to be too vulnerable, be situated at considerable distance from the enemy. Designed to pierce the anti-aircraft system of the latter, they are so costly that only a thermonuclear bomb becomes a load worthy of being carried by them. Furthermore, since the precision firing of a rocket depends necessarily on its range, only an H-bomb has a zone of total destruction sufficiently great to guarantee that the ability of its carrier rocket to reach its objective will not be too greatly affected by its vast range.

The base of a weapon of deterrence is considered to be "hard" when it consists of an underground installation and is protected against explosion. Otherwise it is considered "soft."

The invulnerability of a unit of deterrent weapons depends on a number of factors:

1. The "hardness" of the bases of the elements which comprise the deterrent unit.
2. The efficiency of the warning and anti-aircraft system of the bases.
3. The distance separating the bases from the opponent's positions.
4. The dispersion or spread of the various elements of the unit.
5. Their partial mobility.

The question of "hardness" is an extremely important factor in the invulnerability of a base. An entirely "soft" base is neutralized when situated in the fatal danger zone produced by an H-bomb explosion. A "hard" base on the other hand could be put out of action only if situated in the zone of total destruction.

Studies based on the results of the Bikini explosion, on March 1, 1954, of a hydrogen bomb with an equivalent of 15 megatons of TNT indicated a zone of total destruction (caused by blast wave effect) of circular shape and with a surface area of approximately 93 square miles, plus a fatal danger zone (produced by blast wave, heat and radioactivity) of elliptical shape, with the long axis running in the wind direction and having a length of 220 miles, covering a ground area of approximately 7,720 square miles.

The surface area of the zone of total destruction is thus approximately one-hundredth that of the fatal danger zone.

In an article entitled "The Delicate Balance of Terror," published in the January 1959 issue of *Foreign Affairs*, Mr. Albert Wohlstetter, Associate Director of Projects of the Rand Corporation, expresses the following view regarding the role of concrete shelters in reducing the effects of nuclear bombs:

. . . For example, five half-megaton weapons with an average inaccuracy of two miles might be expected to destroy half the population of a city of 900,000 spread over 40 square miles, provided the inhabitants are without shelters. But if they are provided with shelters capable of resisting over-pressures of 100 pounds per square inch, approximately 60 such weapons would be required; and deep rock shelters might force the total up to over a thousand.

No matter what one may think of figures of this kind, there is no doubt that the "hardening" of the bases of a deterrent unit complex considerably diminishes their vulnerability.

The London *Observer* of October 25, 1959 published a dispatch from its Washington correspondent pointing out that

. . . the United States government was under heavy pressure from certain influential circles to "harden" the bases of the Strategic Air Command in order to "force the Russians to use 25 times more missiles to destroy each base than they need to use at present" and also "if the planes are sheltered, the Russians would have to use most if not all of their rockets to destroy the air bases in the first blow, which would spare the cities.

It appears that most of the strategic bases are still of the "soft" type. This is particularly true of the launching platforms set up by the Americans in Europe in accordance with the NATO resolution of December 19, 1957. They consist of Intermediate Range Ballistic Missiles (IRBM) with a range of 1,500 miles which, set up in Europe, can reach vitally important points within Russia.

Four units, each one composed of 15 Thor rockets, have been installed in England. Two Jupiter rocket units have just been installed in Northern Italy, in South Tyrol. Another Jupiter rocket unit has been set up in Turkey.

But since the Thor and Jupiter rockets, actually the only American IRBM rockets that are already operational, require liquid-oxygen-base fuel, their launching platforms cannot be placed underground. They are therefore highly vulnerable.

They are also vulnerable because of their relative proximity to the presumed opponent. It is obviously easier and less costly to destroy an opponent's base if it is situated a short distance from your own than if it is far away. The Thor and Jupiter bases put up in Europe will be within range of very heavy Soviet surprise attack. In such an eventuality they would have the advantage of a few minutes' warning, which would be wholly inadequate for preparing a retaliatory blow. As a matter of fact it is one of the properties of liquid-fuel rockets that they take a relatively long time to launch.

When an American periodical declared in August 1959 that the Thor rockets set up in Great Britain could be launched within 15 minutes, the British Government felt it necessary to contradict this statement.

We have already pointed out that a deterrent must be able to "be the second to fire." Otherwise it ceases to be a deterrent; it becomes a provocation, an invitation to the opponent to destroy it before it has played the only role to which it is suited, that of firing the first shot.

In point of fact, due to their characteristic "softness," their geographic positions and their incapacity to retaliate promptly, the Thor and Jupiter rockets fall precisely in the category of weapons which, instead of acting as deterrents, are means of provocation.

In the article already referred to, Mr. Wohlstetter writes on this subject as follows:

> . . . Missiles placed near the enemy, even if they could not retaliate, would have a potential capability for striking first by surprise. And it may not be easy for the enemy to discern their purpose. The existence of such a force might be a considerable provocation and in fact a dangerous one in the sense that it would place a great burden on our deterrent force which more than ever would have to guarantee extreme risks to the attacker—worse than the risks of waiting in the face of this danger. When not coupled with the ability to strike in retaliation such a capability might suggest—erroneously, to be sure, in the case of the democracies—an intention to strike first. If so, it would tend to provoke rather than to deter general war.

If one examines the reasons that led to the decision to install launching platforms for Thor and Jupiter rockets in

England, Northern Italy and Turkey and the effects such installations are likely to have on the protection of the West, one is inclined to admit that the Communists are right when they maintain that the strategic concepts of the capitalist countries are in most instances only the result of pressure exercised by armaments manufacturers, rarely corresponding to conclusions arrived at by rational thinking.

However, even if the Thor and Jupiter launching platforms fail to act as deterrents they can, by way of compensation, act to some extent as lightning rods, attracting upon themselves a certain number of bombs which might otherwise be used elsewhere. This in itself could be a decisive factor, provided the number of bombs necessary for destroying the launching platforms constituted a considerable part of the total Soviet nuclear stock. It would seem, however, that this is not so. On the one hand this stock must already be quite large and on the other, due to the "softness" of our missile stations, the number of bombs needed for putting them out of commission would be relatively small. Thus the existence in Europe of Thor and Jupiter bases does not seem to have much bearing on the number of missiles that might be dropped on United States territory in the event of war. This is all the more true because that number would probably be determined to a greater extent by the means of long-range delivery available to the Russians than by the stocks of nuclear weapons in their possession.

What cannot survive an attack certainly cannot deter it. Thus Thor and Jupiter bases which are at the mercy of the attacker cannot have a deterrent effect but on the contrary would make the opponent quite understandably anxious to destroy them at the first favorable opportunity. They increase the chances of war and transform the regions in which they are situated to high-priority targets for the opponent. The missiles intended to destroy these bases would simultaneously destroy great stretches of densely populated areas, some of them among the most important which the Atlantic Alliance is supposed to protect.

We might in this connection recall with considerable interest the words in which Mr. Segni, then Italy's Minister of National Defense, explained before the Italian Parliament on September 30, 1958 the agreement his government had just concluded with the United States for the installation of IRBM bases on Italian territory. As reported by *Le Monde* of October 2, 1958 he declared:

> This agreement comes within the framework of strengthening the military defenses of our country. The installation of these missiles cannot cause anxiety to anyone since it represents a new guarantee of defense of our country's independence and freedom against potential aggression. The fear of possible reprisals by an opponent is unfounded, since the disposition of the launching platforms in scattered areas does not make them highly vulnerable to, or useful objectives of, an opponent's atomic weapons. I believe that this strengthening of our defenses, far from being a danger to peace, constitutes on the contrary the safest possible element of guarantee for peace.

We wonder what, in Mr. Segni's view, might constitute "useful objectives" for Soviet missiles, if a Jupiter rocket capable at a moment's notice of destroying Moscow, Kiev or any other large Soviet population center would not be it!

It is already a fact that the USSR has announced its intention to counter the installation of IRBM missiles in Italy by setting up rocket bases in Albania. In view of their geographic situation it is also unlikely that these rockets will be of the kind "to be the second to fire."

The ideal deterrent would be a device that could *only* be the second to fire. Unfortunately such a weapon has not yet been invented. Indiscriminate installation of equipment capable of firing either the first or the second shot (but the first always much more easily) is highly dangerous; and we cannot remain optimistic about the fate of mankind if governments continue much longer to deter one another. The proliferous spread of devices able to fire *only* the first shot has catastrophic implications.

As we already pointed out, the invulnerability of a complex of deterrent elements also depends on the efficiency of warning

40

and anti-aircraft systems at the bases. All other factors being equal, this efficiency increases in proportion to the distance from the opponent. It will therefore always be very low for bases situated in Western Europe, where missile warning time is bound to remain very short. Recently the press announced the projected construction in Britain of a giant radar system able to give the Americans 15 minutes' and the British four minutes' warning regarding missiles launched from Soviet territory. Today anti-aircraft defenses could bring down perhaps nine-tenths of any plane force taking part in a bombing raid, but this defense system would be powerless against missiles traveling at approximately 9,400 miles an hour.

Also, since the invulnerability of a deterrent can be measured by the number of H-bombs necessary to put it out of action, the deterrent itself must be dispersed as much as possible. The feasible degree of dispersal is suggested by the size of the zone of destruction of the anticipated H-bombs. The destruction we are referring to is more or less complete depending on the degree of "hardness" of the bases. The usefulness of dispersal is advocated by those who recommend a multiplicity of launching platforms. Thus General Gallois, formerly a member of SHAPE, proposes in the November 1958 issue of *Réalités* the installation in France of 400 underground launching platforms. In his view they could be neutralized only by between 5,000 to 25,000 nuclear missiles.

Others feel that the benefits of invulnerability derived from dispersal could be obtained more easily and at far lower cost through mobility of the deterrent elements. As long as a launching site is stationary it constitutes a target for the opponent. To let it move about continuously so that the opponent never knows where it is situated appears to be an excellent method for reducing vulnerability, although the mobility of a launching platform is obviously achieved at the expense of its "hardness."

This theory led to the idea of railroad flatcar- and submarine-based missiles.

To make prompt retaliation feasible, the tendency is to replace liquid-fuel by solid-fuel rockets. The latter have the added advantage that they may be launched from a sheltered, underground site. The relationship between enemy distance and vulnerability favors the adoption of intercontinental missiles with smaller payloads. The mobility factor also prompts the adoption of manageable and relatively small rockets even at the expense of the size of the nuclear warhead they are capable of carrying.

Consequently the rockets designated as Minuteman and Polaris are generally considered the elements which will constitute the hard core of the American deterrent several years from now.

The Minuteman is an intercontinental solid-fuel missile capable of being launched from sheltered underground sites as well as from vehicles and railroad flatcars. It weighs only forty tons and offers great advantages over the intercontinental Atlas and Titan liquid-fuel missiles which require stationary launching sites and weigh over one hundred tons. The Atlas and Titan will soon be operational while the Minuteman will be ready for use only toward 1963.

Polaris is another solid-fuel missile having a range of approximately 1,560 miles. It is designed for launching from a submerged submarine. It is already being put on board atomic submarines.

Pending the readying of the Minuteman, it would seem according to press reports that the American deterrent in the next few years will essentially consist of 700 heavy B-52 bombers, 90 Atlas missiles, 110 Titan missiles and about a dozen atomic submarines each of which is equipped with 16 Polaris missiles.

The nuclear warhead of the Polaris is reported to have the power equivalent approximately to two-thirds megaton of TNT. The nuclear warheads of the Atlas and Titan rockets are said to equal four and five megatons respectively.

In the light of these figures, the American deterrent is already quite impressive. Nevertheless influential circles as well as military, scientific and other groups in the United States are determined that this power shall be further increased. With this end in mind they recommend the continuation of nuclear test explosions. Such testing is said to be necessary in order to check and improve the new "packing" methods of fissionable material, methods which are presumably more efficient and permit better use of the latter. These circles advocate the "repacking" of the existing nuclear warheads. The power of these warheads would thus be increased fourfold without requiring any additional fissionable material. On November 8, 1959, the Washington correspondent of the London *Observer* commented as follows on the views of the circles in question:

> Those who oppose prohibition of atomic tests feel that deterrence requires that at all times until total disarmament or arms control is accomplished, Russia should know that, even after she struck the first blow, Western forces would be able to drop on Soviet targets 3,000 megatons of nuclear weapons—more if fall-out shelters and other passive defense measures are developed, say the opponents of a test ban. This is the explosive force needed to inflict on Russia truly forbidding damage.

For the benefit of those of our readers who are not clearly aware of certain statistics we would like to underscore that 3,000 megatons of TNT represent an explosive power equal to 150,000 times that of the Hiroshima bomb and 600 times that of all the explosives used during World War II.

Because of the great vulnerability of the Thor missiles Great Britain has decided to base its own "deterrent" on an IRBM missile of British construction, the Blue Streak, which because it could be buried underground seemed to fulfill the necessary invulnerability requirements. But because of recent technical advantages in the striking precision of missiles it became apparent that a missile with a stationary base, even though an underground one, if situated at a relatively short distance from the enemy, is too weak to exercise a useful "deterrent" effect.

Because Great Britain is relatively close to the Soviet missile bases and because of the probable precision of these missiles it became apparent that the number of Soviet missiles needed to destroy them would be no larger than the number of Blue Streaks themselves.

Under these circumstances the Blue Streak missiles installed in England would have a provocative rather than a deterrent

43

effect. The British therefore discontinued the construction of the Blue Streak and abandoned their plans for a future system of deterrence based on stationary missile launching platforms. They are considering purchase from the United States of Skybolt air-to-ground missiles which may be adapted for use in British bombers, and also of IRBM mobile-base missiles.

The problem of the invulnerability of a "deterrent" system consisting of mobile-base missiles is a complex one. Mobility can only guarantee a high degree of invulnerability if the missiles are properly dispersed. This is for instance the case in a system composed of submarines armed with Polaris missiles. It may be assumed that the enemy will always remain highly uncertain as to the exact position of the submarines at any given moment, because of the vastness of the seas where they operate. Hence a submarine armed with Polaris missiles seems for the time being the weapon which has the minimum provocative effect in relation to its deterrent effect.

But this ceases to be true once the Polaris missiles are mounted on mobile surface launching platforms. This type of emplacement is intrinsically a soft target and the enemy's uncertainty as to its location will hardly be great. The number of projectiles he will need to seriously threaten destruction of such a mobile missile will be a gauge of his uncertainty, which in turn will increase in direct ratio to the size of the territory over which the missile is able to be moved about; that is to say, the density of missiles in the area over which they move will be smaller. If this density is negligible, the provocation factor will be proportionately negligible because the enemy will be compelled to expend large numbers of missiles to destroy a small number of his adversary's armaments. If on the other hand the density is greater, the provocation factor will increase with it. The number of missiles the enemy must sacrifice in order to destroy the engines of war threatening him will depend in fact on the size of the territory where he knows these engines may maneuver, not on their actual number.

Should the enemy feel there is a major source of danger to him from bases in a relatively small and relatively near-by territory, and should he also feel himself capable of destroying this danger with only limited means, he will naturally be strongly tempted to do just that.

That is why the existing plans for equipping NATO as well as Great Britain with surface-based Polaris missiles are the cause of grave apprehension among many West Europeans. For it does seem that these plans call for vast numbers of engines of war operating in a relatively restricted area. Under these conditions the provocation effects of such a system must indeed be given consideration without being weighed against any additional deterrent effect it may be expected to produce.

In a remarkable article published in *World Politics* for April 1960 Malcolm Hoag of the Rand Corporation has written the following regarding the race between invulnerability and means of attack:

> For example, consider hardening a soft point target in Europe fifty-fold. This would constitute a tremendous change, driving the enemy to perhaps a thousand-fold increase in bomb yield and from air to ground-burst weapons if he is to retain the same high confidence of destroying the target with one weapon. Yet to do so may be possible for him only by changing his bomb, not his delivery system, which does not cost him much. What does change enormously is the incidental damage to the countryside should he attack. In a similar way, protecting the soft target by making it mobile may lead to the same incidental result. Given the enormous area over which thermonuclear weapons spread low over-pressures that suffice for soft targets, one promising tactic for the enemy is to compensate for uncertainty about the precise location of a target by blanketing the suspected area with big weapons. And this obvious counter to simple dispersal of targets is to multiply the number of weapons.

This multiplying of weapons will not present any serious difficulties to the enemy if the areas where the mobile targets are to be deployed are fairly restricted and at a relatively "weak" distance from his own bases. That is why a system consisting of Polaris missiles based in Western Europe seems essentially to have more of a provocative than a deterrent effect.

The discussions now going on in the United States concerning the power potential of a deterrent force throw light on differences of opinion regarding the exact role this deterrent is to play. Some feel that the deterrent must above all be a means of reprisal: the deterrent force must, having survived an attack, still be in a position to retaliate by inflicting maximum losses on the enemy. Others feel that the deterrent must be able to destroy the opponent's means of attack.

In view of the general trend toward "hardening" the bases, this second concept requires a deterrent vastly more powerful than the first.

In the first case the principal targets are the big cities on enemy territory; in the second, the enemy air and missile bases. The advocates of the second concept are obviously guided by the quest for a deterrent capable of destroying, if need be, enemy bases before he launches his attack. They feel that if, as a result of unforeseeable circumstances, there is certainty of the imminence of enemy attack, the deterrent should be in a position to make the first move in order to prevent such an attack. A new term has even been coined to describe the situation. It is said that the deterrent must be capable of striking "pre-emptively." The uninitiated may mistake "pre-emptively" for "preventively." But the experts make the following distinction: a war is "preventive" if undertaken because it is *believed* that the enemy is going to attack; a strike is "pre-emptive" when it is *known* that he is going to do so.

In his profoundly analytical book, *Strategy in the Missile Age,* Mr. Bernard Brodie of the Rand Corporation writes on this subject:

> One school of thought has argued that the American system of defense must be based on the concept of anticipatory or "pre-emptive" attack, that is, an attack provoked by an imminent and certain enemy attack. One wag has described this as the principle of "I won't hit first unless you do." The pertinent question is: what is the probability that such fine calculations can be made to work in practice?

> Unless a government is willing to be the aggressor—in which case it would surely do better to forget about warning and choose its own time to attack—the anticipatory attack implicitly requires that warning be unequivocal. Yet early warning is al-

most certain to be equivocal. Only if the enemy is very clumsy or stupid or both will he signal well in advance his intention to attack.

In the February 1, 1959 issue of the *New York Times* the noted American commentator Hanson Baldwin, comparing the characteristics of the two projected types of deterrent, writes:

> . . . the real debate, bound to increase in volume and tempo, is between the concept of "finite" (its opponents call it "minimum") deterrence, and the concept of "counter-force" strategy (its opponents call it "infinite" deterrence). Should we maintain enough nuclear delivery capabilities merely to devastate and destroy an enemy's cities, or should we maintain a force capable of destroying or "blunting" the enemy's nuclear delivery capabilities—his airfields and bombers and missile emplacements?
>
> For the former task—deterrence by city-busting devastation —critics maintain we now have a great "over-kill" capability, the capability of destroying many times over all of the enemy's principal cities and all of his principal military targets.
>
> For the latter task—destroying or "blunting" the enemy's nuclear delivery capability (our present strategic concept)—the planned Administration program in the years ahead (when Russia emplaces more missiles) is probably too small as compared to estimates of future Soviet capabilities. A "counter-force" strategy obviously must be keyed in part to enemy numbers; numbers spawn numbers and as the enemy's missile and delivery strength increases ours must increase.

The author then refers to the two opposing views on this subject which we quote below.

In a speech given in New York in January 1959, Mr. Malcolm A. MacIntyre, Under-Secretary of the Air Force, declared that in the age of missiles,

> . . . some might draw the implication that our deterrent can rest solely on the possession of forces which, after initial attacks upon us, could survive to assure retaliation by general devastation. . . .
>
> This, I believe, would be a diluted deterrent for the danger of this concept is this: The survival forces that could indeed

effect general devastation are so relatively small that they might not be capable of the substantial destruction of the major military forces of intercontinental bombers and missiles available to devastate us. * * * We must have this capability of destroying our enemy's ability to destroy us, or our deterrent can never be exercised except at the expense of our own destruction and our opponent would know this. * * * We cannot allow the missile age to deflect us from attempting * * * to maintain the capability of neutralizing the bomber and missile forces that could devastate us.

On the other hand General Thomas D. White, Chief of Staff of the Air Force, in testimony to the Senate Armed Services Committee, declared: "There is a growing tendency to believe that a force which has less than the capability to destroy the strategic elements of Soviet military forces will be adequate to deter the enemy." After pointing out the "great danger of altering our national strategic concept to have the capability to destroy only the cities and population of the enemy," the General added: "The United States must be capable of destroying the military power of the enemy. This capability is the foundation of our deterrent posture. This is the only thing that will deter the Soviets from taking aggressive action against our allies and from launching a devastating nuclear attack against the United States."

These statements, though not altogether logical, are significant.

Hanson Baldwin then goes on to describe the views of those opposed to the counter-force strategy, saying:

The opponents say that in the age of the missile and of mobile weapons systems it will be almost impossible, even given surprise attack, to knock out all or even 90 per cent of an enemy's nuclear delivery capability. They point out that, despite our best intelligence efforts, we do not know—and cannot possibly know at the start of war—the exact positioning of the enemy's missiles. (There are some indications, for instance, that Russia is planning to use railroad flat cars, which can be constantly shifted in position, as launching platforms for ballistic missiles.) Moreover, no purely defensive system we can build can possibly be 100

48

per cent effective; once some of the enemy's missiles are launched we shall be clobbered. In other words, no matter what kind of a deterrent we build, no matter if we strike Soviet Russia first (in answer, for instance, to Soviet aggression against our positions in Berlin), we must be prepared in the missile age, if the deterrent fails to deter, to lose millions of people and many of our cities.

They declare, too, that the "finite" or "devastation" deterrent can be just as credible to the enemy—and to our allies—as a "counter-force" deterrent; given either strategic concept we must key our actions to the acceptance of huge loss, and so must he.

The "finite" deterrent advocates say that the key to future successful deterrence in the missile age is not unlimited numbers, but the invulnerability of your retaliatory forces to enemy attack. This, they hold, means widely dispersed "hardened" and hidden and mobile weapons systems, like the Polaris-missile-firing submarine, missile-launching aircraft constantly on patrol, and the Air Force's future Minuteman. It does not mean matching missile for missile. When both sides have achieved really invulnerable nuclear-delivery forces then—and not until then—will a real "balance of terror" or nuclear stalemate be achieved.

The controversy described by Hanson Baldwin is essentially between advocates of increasing the invulnerability of the deterrent and those who feel that priority must be given to increasing the striking force. It would seem that the increasing invulnerability of the deterrents might have a stabilizing influence on the balance of terror, since it would reduce the advantage an aggressor could hope to gain from a surprise attack. On the other hand an increase in the striking force without a correlative increase in invulnerability must inevitably render the balance more unstable by increasing the rewards of aggression (or of "initiative").

"Counter-force" strategy can be defended logically only if the goal is to strike a "pre-emptive" blow, or if the possibility of making war or transforming a conflict into thermonuclear war is considered. Implicit in such strategy is the idea that the deterrent must be aimed at the bases of the enemy's deterrent forces.

This makes sense only if one envisages firing the first shot before the opponent's missiles have left their emplacements.

The statements made in the beginning of 1959 during the hearings before the Appropriations Committee of the U.S. House of Representatives by Mr. Douglas, Secretary of the Air Force, and by General White, Air Force Chief of Staff, throw some light on this problem. When asked what in his view would be the primary targets in case of a general war, Mr. Douglas replied:

> It seems to me that there is a major difference in the situation that exists, depending upon whether you visualize the problem arising through a surprise attack on us, or through some aggression against a part of the free world which might conceivably give us the initiative.
>
> Obviously, if we should have the initiative the priority targets for us to destroy would be military targets, targets representing airfields, missile sites, all installations that pose the great threat to the United States.
>
> In the situation where we have to absorb a surprise attack we would certainly lose part of our striking force, so with a reduced striking force we would be in quite a different position because their military targets would have changed in character to a very considerable extent. Aircraft would have left the airfields on their missions; missiles might have been fired from missile installations, so with our remaining or residual striking power which might be very large, I think it is clear that we would turn toward the problem of doing the greatest damage possible to the country as a whole.

General White gave the following answer to the same question:

> In the case, let us say, of tactical or strategic warning there would be three tasks: One, to destroy the enemy's capability to destroy us—that would be the first priority; next would be to blunt the enemy attack on our deployed military forces and other forces in Europe and in Asia; and, third, systematically destroy the Soviet Union's ability to wage war.
>
> In the case of a surprise attack the mission would be exactly, in my opinion, as the Secretary has stated—to do the

50

greatest possible damage to the Soviet Union as a whole, with attention to applying that destruction in such a way as to do as much damage as possible to their residual military striking force.

Obviously, Mr. Douglas does not share Mr. Segni's ideas on the "usefulness" of missile sites as military objectives.

The nature of counterforce strategy is made even more evident by the statements made by General Power on January 29, 1959 before the Preparedness Investigating Subcommittee of the Committee on Armed Services of the U.S. Senate. General Power is Commander-in-Chief of the Strategic Air Command.

After the General had enlarged on the immense advantages that would accrue to the country starting a war, as well as on the seriousness of the problems bound to arise if the initiative were left to the Soviets, the following exchange took place between the General and Senator Stuart Symington:

Senator Symington: "From the standpoint of what we believe a possible enemy would do, the first attack that he would make on us would be to destroy our capacity to retaliate, would it not?"

General Power: "That is correct. You cannot start a war today unless you have a capability to knock out the opposing strike force, and I would like to mention when I talked about initiative before and this deterrent role, that people should understand that you never must get in the position that you cannot start a war yourself. You always must have a capability to strike first, because obviously if these people thought we never could start a war, why, then they could just take this world away from us, piece by piece, because they would know that as long as they do not strike us, we could never do anything about it so you must have a capability to strike first."

Senator Symington: "So what you are really saying is that it is vitally important to the security of the United States to have on hand and combat-ready modern missiles and modern planes and adequately trained people to handle them, because we will never originate any possible nuclear war; is that correct?"

General Power: "I would say there is little likelihood of it. However, you can never be put in the position that you do not have the capability to strike first, because then, they obviously just take you over bit by bit."

General Power's reasoning would be entirely logical if counterforce strategy could with a single blow totally destroy the enemy's retaliatory capacity. Only in such a case would it be possible to strike first without risking suicide! Otherwise what would be the substantial difference between the effect of a "counterforce deterrent" and that of a "finite deterrent"? According to the view shared by the majority of experts, neither the United States nor the USSR could at the present moment with a single blow annihilate the other's retaliatory capacity. This is the very foundation of the system of balance of terror. If ever this balance were upset cataclysm would not be very far off. In the article already quoted, Mr. Wohlstetter states:

> . . . Suppose both the United States and the Soviet Union had the power to destroy each others' retaliatory forces and society, given the opportunity to administer the opening blow. The situation would then be something like the old-fashioned Western gun duel. It would be extraordinarily risky for one side *not* to attempt to destroy the other, or to delay doing so, since it not only can emerge unscathed by striking first but this is the sole way it can reasonably hope to emerge at all. Evidently such a situation is extremely unstable. On the other hand, if it is clear that the aggressor too will suffer catastrophic damage in the event of his aggression, he then has strong reason not to attack, even though he can administer great damage. A protected retaliatory capacity has a stabilizing influence not only in deterring rational attack but also in offering every inducement to both powers to reduce the chance of accidental war.

Although by and large an increase in the deterrent's invulnerability does exercise a stabilizing influence, it must be stressed that inasmuch as this invulnerability is achieved through decentralization and mobility of the elements of the deterrent, it increases the chances of accidental war. In fact communication with numerous dispersed and mobile elements becomes more difficult, more subject to error—hence a likely cause of accidents.

Finally, the gradual substitution of missiles for bombers

will also result in augmenting the possibility of starting accidental war. At present, if suspicious objects are glimpsed on the radar screen, the H-bomb carrying bombers have orders to leave their bases and fly to their assigned strategic targets, with instructions to turn back after a certain time unless they get further orders to continue their mission. But once a missile has been launched it will be difficult to stop it from continuing on its course. A wide spread of nuclear-warhead-equipped missiles will greatly increase the probability of war by accident.

The basic instability inherent in the balance of terror was made graphically clear when, over a period of many months about two years ago, the United States constantly maintained an airborne alert patrol equipped with H-bombs. That this was admittedly only a small part of its Air Force is not the point. What was significant was the strategy itself. On December 1, 1959 Mr. McElroy, Secretary of Defense, announced that in order to cope with the Soviet missile danger the United States proposed to establish a bomber fleet in permanent state of readiness, to be made up of squadrons of strategic bombers constantly on airborne alert.

The instability of the balance of terror is likely to increase during the next few years. Unless measures for disarmament are taken in the meantime, the striking force that each of the two opponents might use for surprise attack will only increase, and with it the temptation to make use of it. The statements made by General White and General Power indicate that this temptation already exists. The commanding officers of the American Air Force, we feel, hold their fingers all too ready on the trigger. We can only hope this is not the case on the Russian side.

The role played by a deterrent is a very delicate one because it operates in the realm of the mind. As soon as this ceases to be the case it stops being a deterrent, either because it has failed in its purpose or because its possessor has lost confidence in it and has decided to make other use of the elements of which it is composed.

The existence of a deterrent is thus very fragile. It depends not only on the success with which it fulfills its purpose but also on the extent to which one may rely on the instinct of self-preservation, the soundness of judgment and the strong nerves of one's opponent. And to have such confidence is, to put it mildly, paradoxical.

The deterrent can never be anything but fragile, for it is constructed on false and artificial premises. The opponent is pictured as on the one hand thoroughly evil, thoroughly rapacious, and on the other infinitely careful, sagacious and completely in control of his nerves; on these fanciful foundations there arises an ever more monstrous deterrent whose elements are, alas, a stark reality adapted to anything but psychological warfare.

In the praise often heaped on the deterrent while it is glorified as the guarantee of peace one catches the echo of a familiar tune ... July 1914. At that time mobilization was also considered a deterrent. For, as everyone knew, "Mobilization did not mean war."

IV

Limitation
and "Escalation"

THROUGHOUT THE AGES, THE THEORY OF MILITARY SCIENCE HAS considered the purpose of war to be the destruction of the enemy's armed forces.

In the past even partial destruction of a country's armed forces was generally sufficient to render futile a continuation of struggle by its remaining forces, thus allowing the victor to dictate his terms.

In the atomic age the question must be viewed from an entirely new angle. Since the power of a country's armed forces is overwhelmingly composed of nuclear weapons plus their means of delivery, even an infinitesimal part of these forces remains formidable. Consequently war in the nuclear age makes *complete* destruction of the enemy's armed forces mandatory. A single launching platform, a single H-bomb could inflict a fatal blow on many a land. In the future the problem will no longer be, as in the past, how to tip the balance of forces in one's favor. Nothing less will serve than to annihilate the opponent's entire armed power.

Although the advent of the nuclear age has brought about a revolution in essential military concepts, it has produced no similarly profound upheaval in the minds of government leaders entrusted with their countries' national defense. We saw how Mr. Segni referred to the setting up of launching sites in Italy as a "strengthening of the military defenses" of his country. A similar state of mind still seems to prevail among most government leaders. They are unable to see any essential difference between fortifications designed by a Vauban* and bases for long-range rockets with thermonuclear warheads. They still believe they are engaged in national defense when they permit the installation of such bases on the very territories they wish to defend.

For the opponent, these bases are the direct threat; for him they constitute priority targets. Their presence within the borders of the nation they are supposedly defending produces a situation highly characteristic of the atomic age. Indeed, if such bases should ever be installed in a country having a relatively small area and relatively great ambitions of nuclear deterrence, the annihilation of that nation would cease to be a secondary result, a corollary, a by-product of the destruction of its armed power.

The reason is obvious. Thermonuclear bombs with three explosion stages are, due to their radioactive effects, much more efficient for the destruction of a civilian population than an armed force whose main personnel will in the future increasingly consist of rocket operators protected by special devices. For as we have seen the explosion of an H-bomb involves a fatal danger zone one hundred times greater than the zone of total destruction.

In his book, *La Folie des Hommes,* Jules Moch estimated that some fifteen thermonuclear bombs "appropriately distributed" would provide the force necessary for devastating the entire area of France. But if France were to be equipped, as some have suggested, with 400 underground launching platforms dispersed over the entire country, hundreds and probably thousands of similar bombs would be required to destroy her fighting power. France as a nation could thus be irremediably destroyed while her military forces remained in a position to inflict fatal blows on her opponents.

---

*French military engineer (1633-1707) famous for his tactics in the besieging of cities and construction of defense works. Towns attacked under his command were considered doomed; towns protected by his fortifications were reputed impregnable.

We have seen that to the degree that a deterrent is dispersed and made less vulnerable it becomes more efficient. But while governments continue to claim for themselves awareness and concern with the interests of the peoples entrusted to their care, no country's nuclear deterrence policy can appear wholly trustworthy unless it includes provisions for greater dispersal of the population itself, thereby making it less vulnerable. It is not yet entirely unthinkable that a government might desire to protect not only its nuclear bases but also the nation itself. But so long as present thinking prevails, nuclear deterrence policies will remain less efficient in proportion to population density and concentration.

This explains why the British deterrent made up of IRBM missiles installed on the northeast coast of England is hardly reliable. Should war break out, the destruction of these bases would be a high-priority task for the Russians and would result in a disaster of gigantic proportions for Great Britain. Were the wind from the southeast at the moment of attack, the death of probably "only" a few million people would result. If on the contrary the wind blew from the northeast, almost the entire population would perish.

Only nations spread out over very large territories may have some reasonable chance of survival in an atomic war.

Because it is in the nature of nuclear war to compel the belligerents completely to destroy one another's military forces and because the corollary to such destruction must in most instances be the destruction of the enemy nation itself, it is possible if not probable that a nuclear war would result in the mutual annihilation of the two opposing camps.

Aware of the senseless carnage that would result from unleashing nuclear weapons many people feel that by prodding the human spirit into action they may bring about the abolition of war and usher in the reign of peace on earth. Others, more numerous and influential, whose mental make-up precludes all faith in progress and the possibility of elimination of the age-old institution of war, have tried to reconcile the existence of nuclear weapons with war by making the weapons themselves more "humane." Their ideas have a large responsive audience among

57

the ever-growing numbers of persons whose fortune or career depends on the continued existence of armaments and the development of new weapons. These people eagerly embrace the notion that nuclear armaments need not necessarily lead to follies likely to terminate their own lives as well as the existence of mankind.

The motto for a time was, "Mankind must learn to live with nuclear weapons." This seemed all the more inevitable because so many were convinced—erroneously, one might add—that the West was scientifically and technologically superior to the Soviet Union. They saw in nuclear weapons the only efficient defense against communism.

After all, all that was needed was for mankind to learn how to make rational use of nuclear weapons and discover all their hidden qualities.

To place the accent on deterrence turned out to be a stroke of genius. Immediately nuclear weapons appeared endowed with all the virtues. They became the guarantors of peace and were to banish war from our planet forever. The greater the number of these fine contrivances, in fact, the greater would be the warranty for peace. The naive were delighted to learn that henceforth, instead of making war, we would be "making deterrence."

But it soon became evident that nuclear weapons might serve other purposes as well. After all, as long as states do exist they must play politics, and to serve the ends of politics armaments are necessary. Besides, a *status quo* lasting indefinitely is a difficult concept. The right of the strong must prevail without, however, endangering all life on earth. To that end the theory of "limited" war was invented. According to this idea the struggle was to be conducted under a set of well-defined rules; then at a given moment the weaker adversary was to have the extraordinary good sense to come to terms without having had recourse to his strongest weapons.

Finally, all that was needed to divest nuclear and thermonuclear bombs of their all too pronounced massive and blindly destructive character was to start manufacturing "clean" bombs, ones without radioactive effects. The solution of this new problem actually seemed to be in sight—but it required the continuation of nuclear test explosions.

Today there is no more talk of the "clean" bomb; but since it elicited so much interest in the still-recent past we do feel the subject deserves brief discussion.

During the years 1956-1957 the United States Atomic Energy Commission announced on several occasions that American scientists were producing a "clean" bomb free of all radioactive fallout. Such a bomb was to have a vastly reduced fatal danger zone and its effects were not to exceed its military purpose to the same extent as earlier models. There were those of course who questioned the usefulness of all this hard work if the Russians were to continue to be satisfied with delivering "dirty" bombs.

As a matter of fact "clean" bombs, granting they could be produced at all, could indeed serve certain strategic purposes. A region devastated or neutralized by "clean" bombs could be occupied by troops more easily and swiftly than a region devastated by radioactive bombs. But the countries of the West have always tended to believe that, because of the numerical superiority of the armies of the communist countries, the West could not possibly afford to rely solely on conventional weapons and would be forced to make use of the superior power of atomic explosives. Of course, due to the radioactivity factor, there is a vast intrinsic difference between nuclear and conventional explosives. The first belligerent to use nuclear explosives would be assuming the terrible responsibility for inviting The Great Catastrophe. Nor would there be any intrinsic difference between the effects of absolutely "clean" nuclear bombs and those of conventional bombs, so that the use of "clean" bombs would remain within the scope of conventional war.

If the United States were successful in producing really "clean" bombs, it could wage a war with weapons that, while vastly more powerful, could still be considered as "conventional." And it would then be up to the Russians to take the responsibility for transforming the conflict into a radioactive cataclysm.

Some American scientists undertook a frenzied campaign in favor of the continuation of nuclear test explosions, going so far as to label as a crime against humanity any attempt to hinder research work for perfecting the "clean" bomb.

The ordinary atomic bombs, the so-called A-bombs based on the fission process and made either with the Uranium-235 atom (Hiroshima type) or the Plutonium-239 atom (Nagasaki type), are essentially "dirty." The fission reaction releases a host of radioactive by-products, the most injurious of which are Strontium-90 (causing leukemia and bone cancer) and Cesium-137 (dangerous because of its genetic effects).

But the thermonuclear bomb, or the so-called H-bomb, has an A-bomb as detonator. The explosion of an H-bomb thus releases the radioactive wastes of its detonator A-bomb. Furthermore, although the fusion phenomenon of the heavy hydrogen atoms which characterizes the H-bomb does not produce radioactive waste-products, it releases a large quantity of neutrons which, in contact with nitrogen in the atmosphere, yield radioactive Carbon-14.

But the so-called H-bombs are actually three-stage bombs: fission—fusion—fission. The deuteride lithium containing the heavy hydrogen atoms that are to fuse is surrounded by an ordinary Uranium-238 jacket which disintegrates by the fission process when bombarded by neutrons coming from the fusion reaction, and in so doing gives off the same radioactive waste products as the Uranium-235 of the A-bomb. In an H-bomb the A-bomb is used as a detonator for the fusion reaction; and the latter in turn is used as a detonator for the fission of Uranium-238. On an average 80 per cent of the total energy is supplied by the last-mentioned reaction, 15 per cent by that of the fusion process and the remaining 5 per cent by the detonator A-bomb.

It is possible to build an "all-fusion" H-bomb without a Uranium-238 jacket, but this would be very uneconomical. Fusion reaction would cease very quickly, due to the temperature drop following the much larger external heat losses. Besides, such a bomb would always generate the radioactive wastes of its detonator A-bomb as well as, of course, the radioactive Carbon-14 produced through the collision of the neutrons with the nitrogen atoms in the atmosphere. We may rest assured that the H-bombs stockpiled by the big powers are and will remain fission—fusion—fission bombs, that is to say, terribly "dirty" bombs.

Doctor Schweitzer states in *Peace or Atomic War?*:

> The clean atomic bomb is not intended for use. It is reserved for the showcase. It is meant to convince public opinion that future test explosions will produce ever-smaller quantities of radioactive elements; and that clinches the argument against their continuation.

The campaign conducted by Edward Teller and a few others came to an end in April 1958 when General Starbird, an Atomic Energy Commission expert, declared before the Senate Committee, "We see no way of producing a completely clean weapon."

Nevertheless in July 1958 the representatives of fourteen nations were invited to be present at a test explosion of a "clean" bomb in the Pacific. But at the very last moment the demonstration was adjourned *sine die*. Nor has there been any further mention of the matter.

According to newspaper reports that appeared in October 1959, the Russians are said to have invented a new H-bomb not requiring an A-bomb as detonator. It is to be hoped that this piece of news is incorrect. If it were possible to produce thermonuclear bombs without requiring any fission products at all, the problem of the possible control of nuclear weapons would become still more difficult to solve. In any event, however, a bomb containing only fusion elements would not be "economical," nor would it be 100 per cent "clean" due to the production of radioactive Carbon-14.

The question of "limited war," however, is still with us. All the more so because the territory of the United States becomes increasingly more exposed to Soviet rockets. This question is of very great importance, for the belief that a "limited" war is possible may at a given moment exert a decisive influence on the starting of a war.

In the United States the concept of "limited war" has already been the subject of a vast amount of literature. In general it postulates that war cannot be abolished and stresses the need to confine it within certain limits if we desire to avoid the end of life on earth. To avoid being forced to use the most powerful weapons, it is also necessary to have adequate quantities of smaller ones. According to this theory the great deterrents are intended for "limiting" rather than preventing war.

The most famous as well as the most widely read book dealing with the question is Dr. Henry A. Kissinger's *Nuclear Weapons and Foreign Policy,* published in 1957. It came out under the auspices of the Council on Foreign Relations set up three years earlier to study the question. The Council, working as a committee, was under the chairmanship of Mr. Gordon Dean, President of both the General Dynamics Corporation and the Nuclear Science and Engineering Corporation. The Committee held hearings, inviting various personalities, civilian officials and military personnel, experts in the field of atomic science, university professors and businessmen.

After eighteen months of study and discussion the Committee requested Dr. Kissinger, who was one of its members, to write a book for which he would bear sole responsibility and which would be based on the discussions in which he had participated. After completion of the book the Council on Foreign Relations, while stressing the author's exclusive responsibility for the opinions expressed, felt obligated to present them to the public.

The Council on Foreign Relations is a private body but distinctly representative of the ruling circles of the United States. Its president is Mr. John J. McCloy, President of the Chase Manhattan Bank and former United States High Commissioner in Germany. Mr. David Rockefeller is one of the vice-presidents and Mr. Allen W. Dulles one of its members.

In his book Dr. Kissinger concerns himself with the paralysis likely to creep over foreign policy in the face of the monstrousness of the effects of modern weapons. To overcome this paralysis, he believes, strategy must present the policymakers with alternatives less sharply defined than a choice between inaction and total war.

He states in particular:

> . . . The most agonizing decision a statesman can face is whether or not to unleash all-out war; all pressures will make

for hesitation, short of a direct attack threatening the national existence. In any other situation he will be inhibited by the incommensurability between the cost of the war and the objective in dispute. And he will be confirmed in his hesitations by the conviction that, so long as his retaliatory force remains intact, no shift in the territorial balance is of decisive significance. Thus both the horror and the power of modern weapons tend to paralyze action. . . .

. . . Strategy can assist policy only by developing a maximum number of stages between total peace (which may mean total surrender) and total war. It can increase the willingness of policy-makers to run risks only if it can demonstrate other means of preventing amputations than the threat of suicide.

According to Dr. Kissinger limited war may either be war confined to one geographic area, or war not calling on all categories of available weapons, or even war in which the latter are used only against certain well-defined targets.

He feels limited war is essentially a political action whose purpose must be to change the will of the opponent but not to crush him, and to make the conditions of surrender more attractive than continued resistance.

The main argument against the theory of limited war is that it would not remain limited — and the phenomenon of "escalation," or enlargement of the war by stages, could not fail to arise. From retaliation to retaliation, the caliber of the weapons used would constantly increase and the theater of operations grow continuously. The level of total war would soon be reached. Dr. Kissinger replies that this argument is based on the assumption that both parties would look for an excuse to extend the war. In reality they would probably look for every possible reason to prevent a thermonuclear cataclysm. He feels that limited war is possible since the two parties may have one common and predominant interest: to prevent war from spreading. He adds:

The fear that an all-out thermonuclear war might lead to the disintegration of the social structure offers an opportunity to set limits to both war and diplomacy.

Dr. Kissinger says that today's strategy must have at its disposal a whole range of means and methods for coping with the Soviet challenge. It must be able to drive the opponent into situations from which he cannot extricate himself except by starting total war—yet it must continuously try to dissuade him from acting in this manner by maintaining superior reprisal power. He then states:

> Since the most difficult decision for a statesman is whether to risk the national substance by unleashing an all-out war, the psychological advantage will always be on the side of the power which can shift to its opponent the decision to initiate all-out war. . . .

May we be allowed to find somewhat strange a concept of strategy which consists in entrusting the fate of the nation to be defended to the discretion and wisdom of the opponent, whose patience is all the while being tried to the limit through skillful provocation alternating with intimidation.

We noted that the idea of leaving up to the opponent the decision for starting total war was also expressed by General Norstad in June 1959. This seems to confirm the opinion that Dr. Kissinger's ideas very greatly influenced American military circles.

One cannot help feeling that this anxiety and the emphasis placed on the psychological inhibitions likely to beset and paralyze political leaders reflect a sort of eagerness to force their hands. Certain American military circles seem at times to find it difficult to put up with the moderating influence of the White House and to be somewhat impatient for a test of the beautiful tools they hold in their hands.

In the *New Statesman* of December 5, 1959 P.M.S. Blackett, famous Cambridge physicist, writes:

> Since the end of the Second World War there have been three occasions on which, following the western military doctrine of the time, the use of atomic weapons to redress the balance in a limited struggle was contemplated. The western world owes much to the restraint of President Truman that atomic bombs were not used in Korea, and to President Eisenhower that they were not used in Indo-China or during the Quemoy struggle.

It appears that in Indo-China America came very close to using tactical atomic weapons against the North Indo-Chinese forces besieging Dien Bien Phu. . . .

In the *New Statesman* of May 2, 1959 the well-known Labor Party M.P. Richard H. S. Crossman recalls a personal experience:

> Whenever I open a new book on the H-bomb my mind is suddenly shadowed by the memory of an afternoon in the Pentagon. It was four and a half years ago and I was in the office of General Twining who is now Chairman of the Chiefs of Staff but was then head of the American Air Force. I had been listening to a ferocious attack on the ambiguous attitude of the White House to the offshore islands which had then come into the news for the first time. It was one of those translucent fall afternoons that atone for the Washington climate during the rest of the year, and behind the General's head I could see the Potomac and the dome of the Capitol burnished by the sunshine. Suddenly General Twining jumped up, looked out of the window, paused and then said, "One fine afternoon like this and I could finish the job! If only those fellows over there would give the word."
>
> I left the Pentagon so shaken that I made the taxi-man drive me to the Lincoln Memorial. There I stood looking up at the vast figure, austere and yet benign. What would Abraham Lincoln have done, I wondered, if one of his subordinates had talked that way? For the real curse of Western democracy is not the breed of generals—after all, they are only doing their duty by preparing for the next war—but the breed of politicians who have permitted policy to be subordinated to strategy. As a result of this mental and moral surrender, we have reversed Clausewitz's dictum. We now treat diplomacy as though it were the continuation of war by other means, and we are developing a complete pseudo-political science, centered round that fallacious cliché, the Cold War.

It would be incorrect to believe that Dr. Kissinger's position on limited wars could be equated in certain respects with that of the Soviet Union which has always clamored for elimination and prohibition of nuclear arms. The limited war contemplated by Dr. Kissinger is, as a matter of fact, not war limited to conventional weapons but rather limited nuclear war.

Using as a reference scale the power expressed in tons of TNT for the major devices to be detonated, we could classify future war into three general categories. Conventional war could be termed the "war of tons," the most powerful bomb used prior to Hiroshima having been approximately ten tons. Limited nuclear war as contemplated by Dr. Kissinger would be conducted mainly with A-bombs and could be designated as the "war of kilotons." Here let us recall that the Hiroshima bomb was equivalent to approximately 20 kilotons. Finally, total or thermonuclear war conducted by means of H-bomb attacks could be termed the "war of megatons"—the bomb exploded at Bikini on March 1, 1954 representing an equivalent of approximately 15 megatons of TNT.

The general consensus of opinion is that a war of megatons would mean universal annihilation. It is widely believed that in a "war of tons" the Soviets would have superiority, and this possibility is glibly cited to explain away the latter's zeal in clamoring for the prohibition of nuclear weapons. As to the "war of kilotons," the Americans feel that in this category the advantage would be theirs. The weapons to be used in such a war could be considered the armaments of the wealthy, for in small atomic bombs the precious fissionable material Uranium-235 operates inefficiently.

Dr. Kissinger points out why he considers a strategy based on limited nuclear war the most advantageous policy for the United States, why it would offer the USA the most favorable set of conditions:

> . . . If weapons are too destructive, the importance of the industrial potential is reduced because a very few weapons suffice to establish an equilibrium. For a nation with a superior industrial potential and a broader base of technology, the strategically most productive form of war is to utilize weapons of an intermediary range of destructiveness, sufficiently complex to require a substantial productive effort, sufficiently destructive so that manpower cannot be substituted for technology, yet discriminating enough to permit the establishment of a significant margin of superiority.

Later in the text he adds:

In a limited nuclear war dispersal is the key to survival and mobility the prerequisite to success. Everything depends on leadership of a high order, personal initiative and mechanical aptitude, qualities more prevalent in our society than in the regimented system of the USSR.

The validity of some of these contentions is doubtful. Dr. Kissinger also fails to mention other obvious considerations. For instance, if the American strategists are able to contemplate limited nuclear war with so much equanimity, it is because they feel the United States would be spared. Avoidance of the use of H-bombs would automatically preclude the use of long-range intercontinental ballistic missiles, since the H-bomb is the only load worthy of being transported by these aristocrats among vehicles. Limited nuclear war could only take place along the borders of the USSR and her allies, that is to say, in Europe and in Asia.

One of the objections that might be raised to Dr. Kissinger's theories is that even more than is the case with conventional war, there would be difficulty in *keeping* nuclear war *limited*.

With the introduction of miniaturization of atomic bombs there can be no more solutions based on levels of usable explosive power. Some of the atomic weapons are now so small they represent an equivalent of only six tons of TNT. This makes them less powerful than the most powerful among conventional bombs.

In the days when a vast difference still existed between the largest of the conventional bombs (ten tons of TNT) and the weakest atomic ones (Hiroshima type, equivalent to 20 kilotons of TNT), it was easy enough to conceive how two nuclear powers could by tacit agreement restrict the conflict between them to conventional weapons only. There existed along the explosive power escalator a big gap which had to be crossed first.

Such limitation is much more difficult to imagine today, since all gaps along the escalator have vanished. The escalator itself has been replaced by a gently rising ramp.

Nevertheless there still exists an intrinsic difference between conventional and nuclear explosives. Only the latter produce radioactive effects that are immediately traceable. And only a really "clean" bomb could have eliminated this difference. But such a bomb is not possible. Therefore the use of nuclear weapons in a war until then restricted to the use of conventional arms would be a clearly defined action.

On the other hand once we come into the field of nuclear weapons there are no more gaps. Bombs may be manufactured in any desired capacity from six tons of TNT *ad infinitum.* There are no further obstacles along the ramp.

Dr. Kissinger concedes that the great difficulty with limited war is the carrying into effect of the tacit agreement, indispensable to the opponents since they would have to know exactly what their reciprocal intentions are.

To avoid any misunderstandings likely to arise in the heat of battle Dr. Kissinger wants these intentions announced in advance. "Limited nuclear war is impossible," he writes, "unless our diplomacy succeeds in giving an indication of our intentions to the other side. . . ."

Dr. Kissinger suggests that during negotiations for possible disarmament priority consideration should be given to a program for mitigating the horrors of war. This program could help clarify the intentions of the potential opponents and avoid an outbreak of total war by accident. Since strategic striking power provides a guarantee for limiting future war, Dr. Kissinger feels it would be indispensable for air and rocket bases to be secure against all attack.

He writes:

> . . . We might propose that neither bases of the opposing strategic air forces nor towns above a certain size would be attacked, provided these bases would not be used to support tactical operations and that the towns would not contain military installations useful against armed forces. Such a proposal could be combined with the control schemes of the general disarmament proposals. For example, each side could be required to list its strategic air bases which would then be immune from attack. . . .

Dr. Kissinger contemplates the possibility of having inspectors admitted to strategic bases. It would be up to them to guarantee that these bases would not be used for tactical purposes. He also feels that the United States could unilaterally state its interpretation of limited war. In this connection he says:

> . . . we could announce that Soviet aggression would be resisted with nuclear weapons if necessary; that in resisting we would not use more than 500 kilotons explosive power unless the enemy used them first; that we would use "clean" bombs with minimal fall-out effects for any larger explosive equivalent unless the enemy violated the understanding; that we would not attack the enemy retaliatory force or enemy cities located more than a certain distance behind the battle zone or the initial line of demarcation (say, five hundred miles); that within this zone we would not use nuclear weapons against cities declared open and so verified by inspection, the inspectors to remain in the battle zone even during the course of military operations.

The above is indicative of the capacity for daydreaming on the part of advocates of limited war, a capacity that seems simply limitless! Such flights of fancy reveal to what lengths the human mind is ready to go when coping with paradoxical situations. But we cannot let this pass with a mere shrug of the shoulders, for it is this kind of dream that leads to fantastic armaments expenditures. In addition, such extravaganzas prepare minds already superficially inclined to do so to accept the idea of war —war which unfortunately would be a harsh reality.

The weakness of the theory of limited war lies in that it relies on so brittle a concept as the trust which the opponents might place in each other's good intentions. It is paradoxical to assume that a feeling of mutual confidence nonexistent in peacetime would suddenly blossom in time of war. To build such a hypothesis is tantamount to considering war a joint enterprise and the strategists' game the ultimate purpose of nations.

Actually if "limited" hostilities were ever to break out, it is probable that unless they were stopped almost instantly the *escalation* phenomenon could not be prevented. It is equally probable that all the rungs of the ladder would be bypassed in a single stride.

We noted in an earlier chapter the degree of instability of the balance of terror and the immense advantage accruing to those striking the first blow.

Once hostilities have begun, the temptation to unleash the big deterrents without delay so as to outmaneuver one's opponent would quickly become irresistible.

It should also be noted that the policy as well as the strategy of the Western powers has long been based on the concept of *escalation*. Should the Russians attack with conventional weapons the Western powers would retaliate with tactical nuclear weapons. Should the Russians respond in kind, the West would dispatch strategic nuclear weapons to Russian cities, and so on. According to the 1957 and 1958 White Papers a "major" Soviet attack on the Continent, even if restricted to the use of conventional weapons, would precipitate thermonuclear retaliation by Britain against the "sources of power," i.e., against Russian cities.

Moreover, Dr. Kissinger's limited war is a war to be conducted on that rung of the ladder which suits the United States. For that reason it smacks of wishful thinking and becomes unrealistic.

In certain cases limited war is nevertheless possible. The Korean war was a case in point. The Americans refrained from attacking the airfields in Manchuria while the Chinese did not try to restrict the movements of American aircraft carriers or interfere with the activities of American bases in Japan. Indeed no attempt was made to block the Korean ports of Pusan and Inchon which were used by the United States forces. It is probable that, had the Americans bombed Manchuria, the Chinese might have retaliated by attacking Korean ports. This in turn would have forced the Americans into a very difficult situation and would undoubtedly have caused a new *escalation*.

However it was possible to keep the Korean war limited because the framework necessary for such limitation did exist. Just as boiling water in order not to spill must have a vessel to contain it, so a war—if it is to remain limited and not to spread—must have a framework to enclose it. In the case of Korea such a framework did exist. As to the weapons used, they remained restricted to conventional arms because a clear-cut continuity-break separated the conventional from the nuclear weapons at the time. Moreover Korea is a well-defined national and geographic entity within clearly delineated confines. It would therefore be a mistake to offer the experience of the Korean war as justification for entertaining exaggerated illusions regarding the probability of future limited wars.

It should also be pointed out that generally speaking a policy of deterrence tends to make limited war less and less possible. Formal alliances, the integration of armed forces within these alliances and the very existence of tactical nuclear weapons destroy the framework itself within which a limited war could take place.

Since integration of armed forces points in the direction of expansion of war, American proponents of limited war advocate a kind of disintegration of national armed forces as such. Thus some feel that the tactical nuclear power of the NATO Shield should be increased so as to permit this power to wage and win a successful limited nuclear war in Europe on its own.

The proposal to dot the territory of NATO with Polaris missiles whose field of operation would be Western Europe is doubtless at least in part inspired by considerations of this sort. On both sides of the Atlantic there are those who wish to see NATO provided with a formidable deterrent separate from and eventually independent of the great American deterrent. We believe that any system of strategic armaments based in Western Europe would be too vulnerable to have of itself a deterrent effect on the USSR. Its very existence would depend on the deterrent effect of the major American strategic armaments.

This is the thinking behind Dr. Kissinger's advocacy of reorganization of the U.S. Armed Forces by setting up two basic organizations, the Strategic Force and the Tactical Force. He writes:

> . . . The Strategic Force would be the units required for all-out war. It would include the Strategic Air Command, the Air Defense Command, the units of the Army required to protect overseas bases and the units of the Navy which are to participate in the retaliatory attack. The Tactical Force would

be the Army, Air Force and Navy units required for limited war. . . .

This constitutes a tendency to separate the U.S. Armed Forces into two groups, one that would and one that would not participate in a war.

It is highly improbable that an adversary would recognize such a duality. The Russians have always ridiculed the idea of limited war.

This trend toward duality also becomes manifest when certain circles draw a line between matters to be decided by the President of the United States himself and those to be left up to the command in the field.

During the Quemoy crisis in the fall of 1958 President Eisenhower created considerable stir at a press conference when he professed to be unable to answer the question as to who would be authorized to decide on the use of tactical atomic devices. By implying that such a decision might be left to the discretion of a local commander the President undoubtedly wished to reduce the possibility of a situation involving their use to the dimensions of a local incident which need not necessarily result in total war.

With respect to the European situation it certainly is not clear, at least not to the man in the street, precisely who would be empowered to make the decision for the possible use of tactical atomic weapons. Some assert that the decision on such use is left to the discretion of General Norstad. In this connection we can only share the view expressed by Professor P. M. S. Blackett in the article already referred to:

> Military caution would suggest that the attempt to distinguish operationally between tactical and strategic atomic weapons should be abandoned and that tactical atomic weapons should therefore be kept under the same rigid control as strategic weapons; or in the language of deterrence, the little deterrent must be considered in practice as part of the great deterrent.

Europeans should be well aware of the fact that a nuclear war which could be considered limited by the United States would, for them, be total war.

V

Hugging Technique and Disengagement

DREAMS OF LIMITED NUCLEAR WAR ARE CLOSELY RELATED TO the fierce opposition to the various plans put forward in recent years for "disengagement" or "reduction of armed forces" in Europe.

Adoption of any one of these plans would in fact have demolished the framework for that projected limited nuclear war for which some consider Europe a most suitable theater.

Almost three years have passed since the formulation of the Rapacki Plan and we must admit that the hope of seeing it put into action is no greater than it was. This "so reasonable" plan, as Dr. Schweitzer termed it, did at first elicit some favorable reactions in the West. Even the Belgian Government, whose orthodoxy within the Western alliance has never been challenged, in April 1958 described the Polish initiative as a "valuable contribution" to the cause of peace.

But this "valuable contribution" was never followed up. All the powers of Hell were set in motion to reject a proposal that could have saved Europe but that upset the plans of general staffs and loomed as a serious threat to the interests of the host of profiteers of the cold war.

We shall not attempt to air again the history of the Rapacki Plan and the manner in which we succeeded in concealing the truths it contained. Let us merely bring a few salient facts to the attention of the reader.

For many years the Western powers have been asserting that the governments of the communist countries alone were responsible for the armaments race due to their negative attitude regarding the questions of control and inspection necessary for effective disarmament. But the Polish Government memorandum of February 14, 1958, which gave the details of the Rapacki Plan, had this to say on the subject:

> In order to ensure the effectiveness and the implementation of the obligations referred to . . . the States concerned would undertake to create a system of broad and effective control in the area of the proposed zone and submit themselves to its functioning. This system could comprise ground as well as aerial control. Adequate control posts, with rights and possibilities of action which would ensure the effectiveness of inspection, could also be established. The details and forms of the implementation of control can be agreed upon on the basis of the experience acquired up to the present time in this field, as well as on the basis of proposals submitted by various States in the course of the disarmament negotiations, in the form and to the extent in which they can be adapted to the area of the zone. The system of control established for the denuclearized zone could provide useful experience for the realization of broader disarmament agreement.
>
> For the purpose of supervising the implementation of the proposed obligations an adequate control machinery should be established. There could participate in it, for example, representatives appointed not excluding *ad personam* appointments by organs of the North Atlantic Treaty Organization and of the Warsaw Treaty. Nationals or representatives of States, which do not belong to any military grouping in Europe, could also participate in it. The procedure of the establishment, operation and reporting of the control organs can be the subject of further mutual stipulations.

By never following up this proposal, by displaying no desire to enter into discussion with the communist countries regarding the control methods they might be ready to accept, the governments of the Western powers have raised most serious doubts as to the sincerity of their stated desire to bring about controlled disarmament.

Let us keep in mind that the denuclearization zone provided for by the Rapacki Plan comprised on the Western side only the territory of the German Federal Republic, or 94,634 square miles, while it also covered East Germany, Czechoslovakia and Poland in the East, i.e., more than twice that area, or 212,355 square miles.

On the other hand the countries of the East were also ready to discuss with the West the concurrent reduction in the same zone of conventional weapons.

According to the London Institute for Strategic Studies the Soviets now have operational missile emplacements in Thuringia and in the Carpathians.

Had the Rapacki Plan been adopted, these missile emplacements would have had to be pushed back at least 625 and 313 miles respectively. Paris, now 437 miles away from the nearest Soviet rocket sites, would have seen this distance increased to 937 miles.

Of course in the age of intercontinental missiles no distance is a guarantee of security. It is nevertheless true that distance is still a vital factor in gauging the cost and the difficulties involved in the destruction of a target.

In 1936 the head of the French government expressed concern over the prospect of seeing Strasbourg under permanent threat of German cannon. Today the French government disdainfully rejects a proposal for moving rocket bases some 600 miles back from France's territory for the very reason that it wants to allow the Germans to have atomic cannon. . . . That the rockets may be aimed against Paris seems to leave this government cold.

The European Systems of National Defense are devoting a good deal of attention to the problem of anti-aircraft and anti-missile defense. Warning time is extremely short—we have already noted, for instance, that in the case of Great Britain this would be about four minutes for ballistic missiles. Carrying the Rapacki Plan into effect could double these warning periods for London and Paris and triple them for Brussels.

Bear in mind that the Rapacki Plan would have produced far less significant changes for Russian cities. The denuclearization of West Germany would increase warning time for Leningrad by only 30 per cent and for Moscow by 20 per cent.

Does that mean that the Polish plan offers greater advantages for the West than for the East? If so, why did the East submit it?

The answer is that the Polish plan contains no advantages greater for one side than for the other. They are at least as great for the East. The main beneficiaries would actually be the countries situated in the denuclearized zone; and these countries cover a wider area and have a larger population in the East than in the West.

Denuclearization serves first and foremost the interests of the population of the country to be so denuclearized. The Polish government understands this and feels that the interests entrusted to its care are identical with those of the population of its country. This is a rather rare phenomenon in this day and age, rare enough in fact to deserve special mention. The Polish government has demonstrated that it is more deeply concerned with the fate of Polish men, women and children than with maintaining rank, based on possession of nuclear weapons, in the echelon of terror or with whether or not it appears "naked" at international conferences.

If the Rapacki Plan seems to favor the countries within the zone to be denuclearized, this is not because it expects the nuclear powers to assume commitments "not to use nuclear weapons against the territory of the zone or against any target whatsoever on this territory," but rather because there would in the future be no priority targets on this territory for the nuclear powers to attack. Skepticism is doubtless justified concerning the value, in the event of nuclear war, of prior commitments; but it seems reasonable to assume that the belligerents would drop their atomic bombs on carefully selected targets. In the event of nuclear war, however, the only targets having any immediate military interests are those likely to become the source of swift and fierce retaliatory action such as launching platforms for nuclear warhead missiles, airfields on which nuclear-bomb-carrying planes are stationed and finally troops equipped with atomic weapons.

On the other hand installations of long-term military importance only, such as ports, industrial plants, oil wells, etc., are not military targets in a war of brief duration. Therefore nobody could derive any advantage from dropping atomic bombs on a denuclearized zone, at least not in the beginning; there would be much more urgent need for these bombs elsewhere.

Opponents of the Rapacki Plan as well as of all disengagement in Europe like to pose the following question: "What good would it do to have a denuclearized zone in Central Europe if this could be spanned by rockets in a matter of minutes and overrun by motorized army units in just a few days?"

To which we might answer, "What is the point of cramming Europe full of nuclear weapons, thus condemning it to total destruction at the very outset of hostilities, if in the very near future intercontinental missiles are contemplated which will be able to reach any target in the world from any point on earth?"

This question is generally left unanswered, but it would seem the opponents of disengagement feel that limited nuclear war must be given a chance to prove itself.

The fact that adversaries no longer need to make contact in order to strike mortal blows at one another has not decreased interest in ideas of "disengagement." This is particularly true in regard to the question of location of strategic armaments.

All strategic arms, in addition to their deterrent effect, have a provocative effect which increases in proportion to their vulnerability.

Moreover, vulnerability of strategic arms increases rapidly as the distance separating them from enemy strategic bases decreases. The greater this distance, the more difficult it will be for the enemy to knock them out. He will have to expend more and more costly missiles in ever greater quantities to accomplish this. What is more, the precision one can expect from a long-range missile decreases rapidly as distance increases.

Strategic arms with bases close to enemy frontiers are especially vulnerable because in case of surprise attack warning time would be much too short to afford these arms a chance to retaliate before being destroyed. Able only to "strike first," they have for that very reason a heavily accentuated provocative character.

The elimination of strategic arms from certain geographic zones chosen in a way to make it impossible for enemy strategic bases to be too near one another would unquestionably result in increasing the stability of the balance of terror by decreasing the temptation on both sides to "strike first."

This elimination would in no way affect the efficacy of the forces of deterrence and reprisal. The targets for these (urban and industrial centers) are indeed soft, highly vulnerable, widely scattered, and they may be reached and destroyed by a relatively low number of very long-range, low-precision projectiles.

It is nevertheless safe to say that the Great Powers would only agree to reduce their "counterforce" capacity under conditions of reciprocity. The Rapacki Plan took this into account.

The main objection to the Rapacki Plan is that denuclearization of West Germany would bring about the departure from Europe of United States forces, which would rather withdraw to the other side of the Atlantic than see themselves deprived of the atomic weapons which at present are part of their regular equipment. The distance separating the Elbe from the Atlantic Ocean is said to constitute the absolute minimum depth necessary for an American bridgehead in Europe, a bridgehead they would suddenly be compelled to relinquish. Only those *a priori* inclined to it will be won over by this argument. The U.S. Armed Forces are withdrawing neither from Korea nor from Formosa, although these form much more compressed bridgeheads than the Europe proposed by the Rapacki Plan.

Western military circles have long maintained that the use of tactical atomic weapons would facilitate defensive action and favor the side with fewer troops. As it becomes evident that atomic weapons offer offensive potentialities at the very least equal to their defensive qualities, there is a growing tendency to come back to this view. But it so happens that any increase in the striking power of NATO's armies due to their being equipped with tactical atomic weapons has been neatly balanced by similar proportionate arming of Soviet forces without, for that matter, altering the relationship of power of the two camps.

78

In any case the face-to-face presence of armies equipped with tactical atomic weapons, by the very nature of the situation, increases the chances of a single incident swiftly assuming catastrophic proportions. In his report on December 13, 1957 to the Foreign Affairs Committee of the Polish Parliament, Mr. Rapacki with good reason made the point that one of the purposes of his plan was to avoid the danger of "a local dispute or even only a local incident immediately and automatically involving Europe as a whole in a major war." Indeed for an army expecting to be attacked with atomic weapons the best and actually the only means of defense consists in forestalling the enemy's intentions by mingling with his troops so as to make it impossible for him to make use of his atomic weapons without jeopardizing his own armed forces. This is the so-called "hugging technique."

Arming with atomic weapons is above all a factor inducing the opponent to start an offensive, since such action is dictated by the most elementary instinct of self-preservation. For that reason the face-to-face presence of armed forces equipped with nuclear weapons constitutes a particularly dangerous and explosive situation.

The Rapacki Plan would have considerably lessened the chances of war by avoiding this dangerous proximity. It would also have prevented in at least one region the establishment of strategic bases uncomfortably close to either of the potential opponents, thus avoiding, as we have pointed out, the creation of a new source of provocations and danger.

The Rapacki Plan was not the only plan for disengagement to which the West reacted with a demurrer plea. In May 1959 the Soviet government unsuccessfully proposed to Japan the creation of a denuclearized "peace-zone" in the Far East which could have spread to cover a large section of the Pacific. In June 1959 the Rumanian government proposed the denuclearization of the Balkans. To this proposal too there was no response although it met with the approval of Marshal Tito.

Nowhere have the vital interests of the peoples and nations been taken into consideration. In all instances these interests had to bow to decrees based on the daydreams of the strategists of limited war.

The ease with which public opinion throughout the world accepts the reasoning of strategists transformed into reasons of state, no matter how irrational and even absurd such reasoning may be, allows for very little optimism on the subject of humanity's chances to surmount the dangers of the atomic age.

In his speech at the Atlantic Congress in London on June 6, 1959 General Norstad, after referring to NATO's decision of December 1957 to stockpile nuclear warheads, declared:

> What I have just cited was a valid answer to the words and actions of the Soviets in December of 1957. It is, if anything, even more applicable today in the light of the many proposals for restricted areas or, in Mr. Khrushchev's words, "zones of peace," which conspicuously omit the zone whence comes the greatest threat to our European members, the USSR itself.

Does General Norstad really believe that a missile site set up in the Ukraine is more dangerous for Paris or London than a rocket emplacement in Thuringia or the Carpathians? Or does he actually believe that Poland, Czechoslovakia and East Germany are not satellites of the USSR and are thus not "nuclearizable"?

But although the Rapacki Plan has remained a dead letter in terms of concrete achievements, we do feel it has had a great influence in the field of ideas.

Up to a few years ago the intellectuals in Western countries very sincerely felt that it was the USSR which must bear major responsibility for the armaments race and the state of tension throughout the world.

The harsh rejection of the Rapacki Plan, the frightening paucity of the arguments used in this connection, dealt a terrible blow to the faith the intellectuals still had in the "Free World" and its struggle for peace, democracy and a better future.

Up to that time everything had been simple. Everything could be blamed on the Russians. And then the name of Rapacki was heard, and it echoed like a reproach to which there can be no answer.

Because of this name there is an ever growing number of men and women whose minds are grappling with the dreadful realization that in the final analysis it will be our democratic society, our society of parliamentarianism and free enterprise, which will have to bear responsibility for unleashing a cataclysm a thousand times more appalling than any that has yet threatened mankind.

These men have not become communists, since one man's wrongs do not make another man's virtues, but they have lost confidence in their own society, their own civilization and political system. Despairing and powerless in the face of vast forces towering over them, they feel immobilized as they wait for the cupidity of one group, the vainglory of the other, and the folly and lack of awareness of the majority inevitably to accomplish their tragic task.

VI

Bucks and Bangs

The objections raised against the Rapacki Plan, claiming that a denuclearized West Germany would open the door to the invasion of Europe by the conventional armed forces of the East, cannot be taken seriously. Indeed it is unthinkable that purely conventional armed forces should launch an offensive against opponents armed with atomic weapons which can strike in a matter of minutes. In view of the rapid growth of atomic weapons, denuclearization increasingly denotes demilitarization. The nuclearization of armies is a trend that shows no signs of coming to a halt. According to an Act of Congress nuclear warheads still remain exclusively in the hands of the Americans; but the armed forces of all NATO countries are being trained in the handling of arms intended for the launching of the warheads in question.

This nuclearization is also speeded by basic economic considerations. When the world learned in 1945 of the explosion of the first atomic bombs, public opinion tried to find reassurance in the fact that these devices required a fantastic outlay of funds and due to this fact would always exist only in very small numbers. These hopes came to nought for fissionable materials, uranium particularly, have become "plentiful" and bombs are relatively cheap. Today's nuclear weapons are means of destruction and extermination unrivaled in economic efficiency.

The vast expansion of nuclear weapons production is due to their extraordinary capacity for producing "a bigger bang for a buck." Having equivalent power at infinitely reduced volume, nuclear bombs can be transported under incomparably more economic conditions than ordinary bombs. At Hiroshima one plane carrying a single atomic bomb was responsible for the death of 78,150 human beings. In the big raid on Tokyo on March 9, 1945, 279 bombers were needed to drop 1,700 tons of TNT bombs to kill 83,000 persons, not a significantly greater number.

In the case of a thermonuclear bomb provided with a Uranium-238 jacket, maximum efficiency is achieved. *Nuclear Explosions and Their Effects*, a study written by a group of Indian scientists under the auspices of Jawaharlal Nehru, offers the following on this subject:

> . . . It is not enough to say that the efficiency of a weapon system is determined by the ratio—and except in very simple cases it is extremely difficult to assess this ratio in quantitative terms—of the damage inflicted on a target complex and the effort and resources going into the production of the weapons system under consideration. As an illustration, imagine a target complex that requires a concentration of an explosive energy equivalent to, say, 20 million tons of TNT. If this much energy is obtained from TNT the cost would be of the order of 10 billion dollars or about one-third of the U.S. Armed Forces budget; and if it is obtained from a fissile material (assuming that 20 per cent of the material actually undergoes fission during the explosion) the amount required would be about 5,000 kilograms at a cost of about 100 million dollars. However, if one could use natural uranium instead of a fissile material, the cost would be about a quarter million dollars.

> It is, of course, absurd to ignore the means of delivery in comparing the relative effectiveness of conventional high explosive bombs with nuclear weapons, but ignoring this factor only serves to emphasize the extraordinary "cheapness" of nuclear weapons as compared to conventional weapons. The mere factor of bulk would make the means of delivery of nuclear weapons enormously more practical and more economical than conventional weapons for the same target effect.

> . . . For the same money and effort nuclear weapons, as compared with conventional weapons, give thousands of times (if not more) larger yield in terms of target damage.

It therefore marked a decisive advance in nuclear weapons when it was realized that in a megatons explosion one could employ Uranium-238 as the source of most of the energy. If one could use Uranium-238, one could also use natural uranium, but it is more economical to use Uranium-238 which is the residue left after most of the very expensive Uranium-235 has been extracted from it in thermal diffusion plants and nuclear reactors. . . .

Not only has the cost of fissionable material gone down but production has also become abundant. The total production of fissionable material for the United States, consisting mainly of Uranium-235, is estimated at more than 50 tons per year, making it possible to manufacture tens of thousands of bombs a year.

Regarding this abundance of fissionable material General James Gavin, until less than two years ago head of the Research Development Department of the United States Armed Forces, stated in his recently published book, *War and Peace in the Space Age*:

> . . . Fissionable material is becoming available in such abundance that the economics of the situation alone will soon compel its use as replacement for the tons of high explosives and steel shells used in the gunpowder era. . . .

And here is General Gavin's prognosis for the future of nuclear arms:

> Nuclear weapons will become conventional fire power. . . . To say that they will become conventional means that they will be in the hands of all military organizations including, for example, the smallest infantry units.

> The United States and the USSR will have in their stockpiles an abundance of large-yield thermonuclear weapons. More significant than these, however, will be the stockpiles of small, precise-yield weapons suitable for tactical employment. Their number, size and performance will be critical to the outcome of any future limited wars.

> Nuclear weapons will become conventional for several reasons, among them cost, effectiveness against enemy weapons, and ease of handling. . . . Many millions of dollars spent in the manufacture, shipping, storage and handling of high-explosive

projectiles and bombs will be saved through the use of nuclear weapons moved by air to combat areas. . . .

Tactical nuclear weapons will be used by individuals in defense against, for example, tank concentrations. In this they may be shoulder-fired. . . . They will be used in air launched missiles. . . .

Abundance of fissionable material has made it possible to earmark part of it for very small atomic weapons in which the explosive substance is utilized with minimum efficiency.

We know that fissionable material splits spontaneously when the quantity of matter present in a single bloc reaches the critical mass, that is, when the neutrons produced by the fission of the atoms within the mass exceed in number the neutrons escaping from the mass to the outside and a chain reaction is produced.

Every bomb must contain a quantity of fissionable material greater than that of the critical mass. The efficiency of the bomb will be proportionately greater as the quantity of material present appreciably exceeds the critical mass. In fact the chain reaction ceases as soon as the mass of unsplit material drops below the critical value. It follows that in every atomic bomb a quantity of fissionable material at least equal to the critical mass remains untransformed into energy and is thus wasted.

Small atomic bombs contain an amount of fissionable material only slightly exceeding that corresponding to the critical mass; hence they are rather inefficient.

Technical writers differ regarding the critical mass for Uranium-235. This apparently depends on the form given the mass. It may be greatly reduced by subjecting the material to pressure. Some writers speak of one kilogram as the approximate value for the critical mass. Others claim that the lowest possible value is 254 grams. If that is so, 254 grams would constitute the minimum quantity of Uranium-235 lost in each atomic weapon.

These inefficient atomic arms answer certain military needs, such as anti-aircraft defense and short-range use on the battle-field.

In addition to the reasons cited earlier in the text in favor of nuclearization, there is still another consideration, derived from the development of the means of rocket delivery. While becoming faster as well as more accurate and complex, these means become more and more expensive.

At the end of World War II a heavy bomber of the B-29 type cost $600,000. Today the B-52 intercontinental jet bomber costs eight million dollars. There is even some talk of a new plane, the X-15, which is to cost one hundred million.

On the other hand, although a Pershing rocket with a range of 500 miles costs only half a million dollars, the Atlas intercontinental missile costs an estimated 17.5 million.

It is quite understandable that such vehicles can be used only for carrying weapons with power proportionate to their costs, i.e., nuclear arms.

VII

Penguins and Seals

There are those who believed the armaments race would come to a halt of its own accord once it became obvious that each of the antagonists was generously equipped with the wherewithal for annihilating his opponent. Nothing of the sort happened. And it has become clear that unless common sense energetically intervenes, the future promises unlimited scope for the armaments race—or rather, prospects that are limited solely by the catastrophe which sooner or later, whether due to mechanical or human failure, cannot fail to overtake us.

The argument in favor of the dispersal of strategic bases carries with it a plea for their increase. The argument for hardening the bases automatically incites the opponent to increase the scope of *his* means of destruction. Finally, within the framework of the general folly, we hear powerful arguments in favor of adopting large-scale shelter construction projects for the benefit of the civilian population.

Thanks to the policy to which we are committed, markets for such industries as concrete, fissionable materials, lithium deuteride and weapon delivery vehicles have become limitless. This is also true for the industries capable of manufacturing tactical and small atomic weapons intended for eventually equipping the artillery arsenals and infantry units of the world.

Year by year all over the world the role assumed by the armaments industry tends to increase and with it grows the influence this industry exerts on the conduct of international policy.

One school of thought which still retains some adherents believes that peace may be safeguarded by powerful armaments, provided these are subject to rigid international control. According to this concept individual states are to retain their defense potentials, but international inspection is to guarantee that these potentials are not utilized for purposes of aggression.

The "open skies" concept derives from this theory and until recently general opinion on this subject assumed that aerial inspection could embarrass only an aggressor, while protecting the possible victim of aggression.

But we must not lose sight of the fact that today all aggressive action would risk provoking counteraction by massive engines of destruction. It is no longer possible for such action to take any form other than that of surprise attack directed against the bases of such engines.

An "open skies" system might be helpful in controlling either total or partial disarmament of certain areas, but applied to territories providing strategic bases it would seem more likely to provoke surprise attack than to forestall it.

Stability of the balance of terror depends in fact on both adversaries being convinced of the impossibility of putting *hors de combat* by means of surprise attack either the total or the near-total deterrence force of the enemy. This conviction will be strengthened as strategic bases seem less vulnerable.

A military command will be less prone to contemplate surprise attack if:

1) enemy strategic bases seem to it hard to destroy;
2) its own strategic bases seem sufficiently invulnerable to be capable of surviving an initial blow delivered by the enemy.

Aerial inspection is by its very nature obviously likely to increase the vulnerability of bases; consequently it will strengthen the reasons of both sides for wishing to be the first to strike.

In the past a surprise attack would have first necessitated troop movements and other preparation of considerable duration. Under those conditions aerial reconnaissance was likely to furnish useful information for preventing attack.

But today a surprise attack would be conducted with strategic arms whose avowed objectives are deterrence and possible retaliation. These arms are maintained in a state of constant alert and, to the extent that this is possible, in readiness for instantaneous action. A surprise attack no longer requires lengthy preparations of the kind which once made such preparations liable to detection via aerial inspection.

An "open skies" system would be in logical contradiction to a system based on the principles of deterrence. Its effect would actually be to weaken the deterrent forces by making them more vulnerable.

Aerial inspections agreed to by everyone might indeed be more frequent than the occasional U-2 flights but they could never guarantee permanent supervision nor detect change-over of armaments from a deterrent to an aggressive function.

It is conceivable that at some future date it will be possible to establish a permanent system of supervision based on a number of satellites of the Midas and Samos type, capable of detecting missiles as these are fired. But it is to be feared that such a system might become a source of errors and accidents with lethal consequences. Yet it is not ruled out either that such a system, by increasing warning periods, would strengthen the stability of the balance of terror rather than weaken it, in the way aerial inspection flights now possible are likely to do.

It is not necessarily true that aerial reconnaissance must serve defensive ends only. A state weighing the possibility of launching a surprise attack must first as accurately as possible determine the location of the objectives it will try to reach, that is to say, first of all, the strategic bases of the enemy. To that end aerial reconnaissance might prove very useful indeed.

Conversely a country determined never to strike first would be less interested in learning the exact location of its enemy's strategic bases.

The targets assigned to such a country's armaments would not in fact be primarily enemy bases, for these would for the most part have been emptied of their murderous contents at the moment they were due for the retaliatory attack. With whatever armaments were left after it had absorbed the enemy's first blow, such a country would be compelled in all logic to try to inflict the greatest possible retaliatory damage by aiming at the enemy's urban and industrial centers, vulnerable targets whose locations are general knowledge.

Once we admit that control of armaments in general, and of strategic arms in particular, cannot provide guarantees for keeping the peace, it becomes all the more important to follow the road of disarmament and disarmament control.

No rational person can possibly believe that the armaments race in its present form is compatible with the maintenance of long-term peace and it is difficult to argue the fact that, confronted as we are by the fantastic development of the means of destruction, general and total disarmament has become the most pressing, in fact the indispensable goal to pursue if we want to avoid the total destruction of mankind.

But we should try not to underestimate the great difficulties and complexities of the problem.

In a report to the U.S. Senate Foreign Relations Committee by the Foreign Policy Research Center of Johns Hopkins University made public on December 6, 1959 we read:

> Maximum disarmament, down to the level of national police forces, is not synonymous with maximum stability and may in fact be inconsistent with it.
>
> In a totally disarmed world, even a small number of secreted or clandestinely manufactured nuclear weapons could disrupt the international order and allow one power to dominate its more trusting adversaries.
>
> It is doubtful that any devisable, much less agreeable, inspection system could disclose such violations with a sufficient degree of certainty.

It is obvious that the more radical the disarmament agreement finally arrived at, the smaller would be the contingent of forces which must be kept hidden in order to guarantee complete dominating power.

This is an undeniable fact which the advocates of disarmament cannot fail to take into account when they elaborate plans of action. Only a disarmament program not involving any risks stands a chance of coming to fruition.

When it comes to manufacturing more arms, any and all risks are permitted; but we are not allowed a single one if it is a question of disarmament.

The buyer of arms enjoys favorable public opinion and no one speculates on the uses to which these weapons are to be put. On the contrary, those advocating arms reductions meet with distrust from the very beginning and their intentions are closely scrutinized.

It is much easier for A to give weapons to B than to come to an agreement with him for the reduction of arms. At a press conference in 1958 United States Secretary of Defense McElroy went so far as to contemplate supplying "clean" H-bombs to the USSR.

It may seem strange that countries which have never fought one another should so fear to conclude disarmament agreements, while with all eagerness they hand out weapons to others with whom they had been at war repeatedly in the recent past. But the armaments race does not take into account logical considerations. The advocates of disarmament cannot afford to depart from strict logic. The interests related to the manufacture of armaments have become so vast, so all-powerful and widespread that only a disarmament program that is crystal clear and formulated with impeccable consistency stands any chance against them.

The same considerations which have stood in the way of any substantial progress in disarmament negotiations in the past few years mitigate against any optimistic approach to the possibility of total disarmament in the near future. They are inescapably connected with the difficulties inherent in the control of nuclear disarmament.

Control of fissionable material plays a vital part in such disarmament. Precluding unforeseen developments such as the invention of an H-bomb not requiring an A-bomb as detonator, fissionable material remains indispensable for the manufacture of nuclear weapons. Yet while plants manufacturing this material itself are of necessity huge and difficult to conceal, plants using it for manufacturing weapons may be rather small and difficult to detect. Furthermore the technique for its manufacture is complicated and highly advanced while that for the manufacture of arms with a fissionable material basis is relatively simple. Finally "fusionable" material, the lithium deuteride used in the composition of the H-bomb, is produced by electrolysis with relatively small and easy-to-conceal equipment.

Consequently control must apply to the *production* of fissionable materials.

To be effective, nuclear disarmament control must be able to:

1) detect any nuclear test explosion;
2) make certain that none of the fissionable material produced is used for military purposes;
3) check that all existing stocks of nuclear weapons are destroyed and that all fissionable materials have been converted to peaceful purposes in accordance with the provision of the disarmament agreement to be concluded.

For almost two years now a conference composed of representatives of the three great nuclear powers has been meeting at Geneva, studying the possibilities for enforcing the first of these conditions. The results are fairly satisfactory: it has been established that it is possible to detect almost all nuclear explosions by means of a certain number of control stations and the three powers are practically agreed on the control methods to be used. Only the question of small underground explosions whose detection appears to be more difficult still constitutes the stumbling block preventing the conclusion of an agreement on control for ending nuclear testing.

The second condition is more difficult to fulfill. According to the experts, and to Mr. Jules Moch in particular, international control of fissionable materials and nuclear power plants could provide a guarantee of only up to 97 per cent that the materials produced would not be used for military purposes.

The Uranium-235 produced in isotope separation plants can be used for peaceful as well as for military purposes and the quantities produced could be determined within a three per cent margin of error only. The same would be true for Plutonium-239 and Uranium-233 produced in nuclear power plants, with both being capable of being put to either peaceful or military uses.

This possibility of clandestine diversion to military purposes of three per cent of fissionable materials can be a most serious factor in view of the huge production potentials of certain countries. As mentioned earlier, annual production of Uranium-235 in the United States is estimated at some fifty tons. So far no international control system has been devised that could detect the diversion of a quantity of one and a half tons per year. To grasp fully the importance of this factor we must bear in mind that such a quantity represents 185 times the eight kilograms of Uranium-235 believed to have gone into the composition of the Hiroshima bomb. Furthermore, technical progress now makes it possible to use fissionable materials in bombs much more economically than in 1945. Finally, much greater destructive power is achievable by using "diverted" fissionable material. We must not forget that the "fusionable" material which goes into the H-bomb is much less costly to produce and above all much easier to conceal than the production of fissionable materials itself.

Diverting three per cent of the fissionable material produced would permit any country with an appreciable production potential rapidly to build up formidable clandestine destructive power.

The possibility for fulfilling the third condition is slighter still.

In some countries production of fissionable materials has been going on for so many years and sometimes under conditions of such secrecy that it is impossible to estimate with a real degree of precision the size of existing stocks. Experts who feel that an international control system could estimate within only a three per cent margin the production taking place within the control period believe that the margin of error for evaluating past production, that is, production carried on before the setting up of controls, would be about 20 or even 30 per cent.

In his *The Arms Race,* referred to earlier in the text, Philip Noel-Baker mentions that Dr. Ralph Lapp, former adviser to the U.S. Atomic Energy Commission, declared several years ago that the A- and H-bomb stocks already existing in the United States were equivalent to some 10,000 megatons of TNT. Twenty or 30 per cent of such a stockpile would be sufficient for the destruction of all the nations on earth.

A satisfactory solution of nuclear disarmament control is unfortunately not in sight; but this does not mean that we must remain passive in the face of our present catastrophic situation or should permit the stockpiling *ad infinitum* of nuclear weapons by either side. No possibility for the reduction or limitation of nuclear weapon stockpiles should be neglected. Any single existing nuclear weapon can trigger a cataclysm.

The International Atomic Energy Agency with headquarters in Vienna was created by the United Nations to assist in the development of nuclear energy throughout the world. Its purpose is to check that no enterprise receiving assistance from it should serve military purposes. It had been proposed that the powers of this agency be enlarged and its funds increased so as to enable it to exercise control over the production of fissionable materials in all countries. In 1957 Mr. Jules Moch estimated that 3,000 inspectors would be needed for this purpose.

As to existing stockpiles of nuclear weapons, it has been proposed that they be made into an international stockpile guarded by United Nations armed forces. This stock would be supplied by the signatories in proportions to be determined (this is the crux of the main problem) and would equal 40 per cent of the stock of the best-supplied power. The establishment of such an international arsenal would serve to discourage clandestine national stockpiling.

It is to be hoped that failing an agreement on their complete elimination, the major powers will find ways to reduce or limit them. But due to the element of uncertainty inherent in the problem, it will be very difficult to find even an imperfect solution. The power best supplied with fissionable materials will lean toward control of the means of production while the others will prefer destruction of existing stocks.

But there is another area where, it is to be hoped, greater progress may be made in reducing the appalling insecurity of the modern world.

Nuclear weapons are difficult to control because of the small quantity of fissionable materials necessary for manufacturing them. But a nuclear bomb *per se* is ineffective—inoperative without the means for letting it reach its destination.

Among the most dangerous means of delivery—dangerous because they are the ones most likely to unleash universal conflagration—are the long-range vehicles capable of penetrating to an adversary's vital centers. Fortunately they are bulky and hence difficult to conceal. We have already mentioned that an Atlas missile weighs over one hundred tons and the Minuteman is to weigh over forty. Bombers are likewise items of imposing size.

It is in the field of the control and elimination of the means of delivery that it is now possible to fight most effectively for the maintenance of peace.

Philip Noel-Baker writes in this connection:

> . . . it has been widely recognized by men in authority that the problem of nuclear aggression, which threatens the future existence of mankind, could be solved if the "means of delivery" required for nuclear weapons were abolished. And all the "means of delivery," bombing aircraft, missiles, aircraft-carriers and submarines, are, in themselves, weapons that help attack against defense; they are weapons that favor surprise and encourage intending aggressors to think that a sudden and unprovoked attack may rapidly succeed. . . .

> . . . neither their manufacture nor their construction, nor their tests, nor the training of troops or crews to use them, could be concealed from UN inspection teams. If they were abolished, the temptation to a disloyal government to divert fissile material to weapons, or to retain a secret stock, would be virtually removed. If the governments genuinely desire to eliminate the danger of nuclear aggression, this is the most important single measure they can take.

On October 22, 1959 Mr. Jules Moch, speaking on behalf of France in the discussion on disarmament before the United Nations Political Commission, stated that any disarmament program "would have to give absolute priority to measures prohibiting first the increase and next the manufacture and stockpiling of carriers for nuclear devices."

In recommending that disarmament efforts start with the elimination of the deadliest of the universal destruction carriers, the French delegate cited the following: satellites, rockets, supersonic or long-range airplanes, airplane carriers and launching platforms.

Most certainly Mr. Moch's proposal reflects in particular the interests of France, which is not likely in the foreseeable future to build many efficient long-range "means of delivery" for the nuclear bombs she very soon counts on having. The French proposal is nevertheless in the interests of all and it is to be hoped that it will be given serious consideration.

We know the long-standing quarrel between East and West regarding disarmament. When the former says, "No control without disarmament," the latter replies, "No disarmament without control."

Certain ingenious minds have tried to solve the impasse by segmenting the proposed disarmament schedule into stages sufficiently small so that the question of whether control is to precede disarmament, or vice versa, would not make much difference.

According to Mr. Moch's plan there would be an initial stage during which the international organization would have no other task than "the gathering of information supplied by all powers, without any control on the spot." This would be "the phase of statements on limitation and would have a psychological effect as a start." During the second stage "the control agency would carry out inspection in accordance with measures then already in effect. Not until the third stage would controls be fully operative."

Obviously, however, it would be difficult to undertake inspection tours for the purpose of listing armaments reductions effected during the first stage without simultaneously gathering information regarding armaments whose elimination is planned for later stages.

The full scope of the difficulties becomes apparent when we read in the *Observer* of November 8, 1959 the following statement from its Washington correspondent:

> . . . the West must not lose its deterrent power until final disarmament is achieved, but on the contrary, as each category of weapons is controlled or eliminated, the remaining weapons must be stronger than before.

In his speech of September 18, 1959 before the General Assembly of the United Nations Mr. Khrushchev said:

> It is necessary to set up a control system for all disarmament measures to be applied in accordance with the disarmament stages.

> If disarmament is comprehensive and complete, then upon its attainment, control shall likewise be general and complete. The states will have nothing to conceal from one another any more. None of them will dispose of a weapon that could be used against the other, and therefore the controllers will be able to manifest their zeal to the full.

The difficulty actually lies in how to exercise control before achieving disarmament, that is, during the period when the various states still have things to hide.

Every system of disarmament by stages in which inspection and control must occur at sites likely still to be of interest to intelligence agencies is destined to encounter great difficulties.

These difficulties might be avoided if instead of a disarmament process, each stage of which constitutes partial disarmament of the entire territory of each of the parties concerned, a method could be chosen that would result in total disarmament of a fraction of that territory, leaving the status of the remaining areas unchanged. Instead of elimination by stages of various categories of armaments over the entire national area, the parties concerned would free by stages various sections of their territories of all armaments whose liquidation would have been agreed upon. Thus disarmament stages would no longer refer to armament categories but to territorial sections. In lieu of disarmament gradually proceeding in depth we would have disarmament gradually spreading across the land.

At regular intervals a portion of the territory of each of the parties involved could be opened for inspection and control by the international organization.

The stages could be as brief as desired. Disarmament could immediately be followed by control over the area just cleared. For instance, if disarmament could be achieved within a period of four years, plans could be made for inspection and control each month by the international organization of a new section representing 1/48th of the territory of each of the parties to the agreement.

There would be no need for long negotiations to establish the sections over which disarmament would extend at each stage. Each of the parties exercising its full sovereign rights could decide which portion of its territory would be disarmed next. The only condition to be met would be that each portion represent the proper fraction of the total surface area. At each stage each of the parties would disarm that portion of its territory which it considered least useful for keeping properly equipped.

Such a method for disarmament of the ground areas would moreover be most logical, for in this age of plentiful nuclear and thermonuclear weapons the ground constitutes the essential factor in the war potential, the only one in fact still well defined and inextensible. In the entire armaments arsenal there is not a single carrier—neither submarine, airplane carrier nor future satellite — that could function indefinitely without the services of ground bases.

A disarmament system progressing along the ground could be adjusted to fit any scale of disarmament desired. Should the powers decide not to go as far as total disarmament, each of them could reserve for itself exclusive control zones intended for use as strategic bases. Yet even such partial disarmament would be a long step in the right direction, for by reducing the surface area of the zones where the spark that might cause war can be ignited, the very chances for setting off that spark would automatically be reduced.

Furthermore by restricting the areas where surprise attacks could originate, the regions constituting high priority targets for the opponents are simultaneously defined. In this way disarmament by stages, progressing over ground surfaces, even before reaching the phase of total disarmament, could both reduce the chances of precipitating a cataclysm and limit the scope of the regions marked for destruction in the very first hours of conflict. Thus even were war to break out, mankind would still have the opportunity to regain possession of its senses and to call a halt to the disaster before all life disappeared. It would yet be given an alternative to destroying itself, saying as did Kaiser Wilhelm in 1914, "This is not what I intended."

If, as we feel, a system of disarmament by stages, ground sector by ground sector, is the one that has the best chance of being carried into effect in practice, then certain aspects of local disarmament must be considered useful and even necessary steps toward general disarmament. We feel that the road to total disarmament is through the setting up of such zones of local disarmament, and whether this takes the form of denuclearized, reduced-armament or completely demilitarized zones does not matter.

One may wonder how best to start the process of gradual disarmament of ground surfaces. Use can be made of the fact that regional disarmament is above all in the interests of the local inhabitants who would thus cease to be a priority target for massive destruction weapons.

It is said that "function creates the organ." It is not less true that often "the organ creates the function." The role of armaments in the genesis of wars is a striking example of this.

We must therefore hope for the promptest possible setting up by the United Nations of an international body whose task it would be to inspect and control the armaments of any state requesting it to do so. It is to be fervently hoped that such a body may be set up before a concrete reason for its activities is provided by the needs of any one country. Once this body has been made a reality and cadres of international inspectors are operating, it is probable that not much time would elapse before one or another country appealed to it for help, hoping to find in it guarantees of safety and protection. We must not make the mistake of assuming that any country, irrespective of the peaceful intentions of its leaders, is a potential surprise aggressor and is to be considered as such if it harbors on its territory carriers capable of long-range transportation of the means of massive destruction.

A country not harboring such carriers and hence incapable of participating in a surprise attack would find it distinctly advantageous to have this situation officially and internationally confirmed. Universal certainty that a given territory cannot be utilized for unleashing a surprise attack would mean for its inhabitants as solid a guarantee of security as it is possible to have until the time when general total disarmament can be brought about.

This fact, internationally recognized, would constitute reliable protection against erratic intervention by other states and against pressures on their part to compel a country to change its policy and join either of the military blocs.

The first state willing to take the initiative and declare that it renounces the right to possess the means for long-range delivery of massive destruction devices, that it refuses to permit other states to make such installations on its territory and offers permission to the representatives of any nation to check on the non-existence on its territory of any such installation, at the same time requesting the creation by the United Nations of an international body empowered to certify its inability to participate in a surprise attack, would render a tremendous service to the cause of peace while also serving its own best interests.

It would be difficult for a country committed to a policy of military alliance to take initiative of this nature, but all over the world there are countries that could do so and would, moreover, find the doing greatly to their advantage.

On December 27, 1959 a committee appointed by the Advisory Council of the United States Democratic Party under the chairmanship of Dr. Ernest C. Pollard of Yale University declared itself in favor of "total elimination of the major tools of sudden mass destruction" and of general disarmament, possibly down to the level of ordinary police forces. The committee's report emphasized that "human error or mental confusion could trigger a nuclear war." The report also exposed the dangers likely to arise from the distribution of nuclear weapons to a great number of countries, noting in this connection that "a nuclear-armed Cuba could threaten the United States."

Now Cuba is a country which would find it in its own best interest to be given a certificate by an international body testifying to its inability to participate in a surprise attack. There are others, such as Finland and Yugoslavia. Neither camp possesses bases in these countries. They do not therefore constitute targets for arms of massive destruction and consequently the populations of these countries enjoy a privileged position in Europe today. It would be in their interests to crystallize this position.

We see therefore that controlled disarmament or some lesser control over certain weapons might very well be put into practice and gain ground as a result of unilateral decisions taken by governments that are concerned with the best interests of the inhabitants of their countries. This does not necessarily apply exclusively to countries which pursue an independent policy and owe allegiance to no great nuclear power. It is for instance conceivable for a member state of a nuclear military bloc to request of the United Nations certification as to incapacity to participate in a surprise attack for some section of its territory whose value from a strategic viewpoint is insignificant compared to its value from a "civilian" point of view. It is for instance not impossible to imagine that the Italian government, fully cognizant of the fact that the Vatican State is surrounded by its territory and that the Holy See is a point of interest for Catholics all over the world, would request for a part of central Italy a "reduced arms" certificate that would protect Rome from becoming a priority target for massive destruction devices. It would be equally possible for the government of Greece to undertake similar action regarding Athens, this cradle of Western civilization that runs the risk of being destroyed under the pretext of being defended. Other governments could take similar action for areas they valued too highly to permit the installation of strategic bases on them.

It is to be feared that the zones of peace and areas with at least "reduced armaments," set up by unilateral decision, will extend over only rather limited areas inasmuch as the surface area of the territories available to military blocs constitutes an essential factor in their strategic potentialities. But due to the advantages their inhabitants would derive from their very existence, the setting up of these zones might act as an example likely to prompt the military blocs to start on the road of gradual and reciprocal disarmament of other territories.

In view of the bulk of carriers capable of transporting nuclear devices over great distances, control over their elimination is not likely to raise insurmountable difficulties.

A guarantee given by an international body as to a state's inability to participate in surprise attacks would require permanent inspection by international agencies not only of its airfield but also of its points and means of entry, such as highways, railroads and seaports. We must remember that a few years from now, when mobile and solid-fuel propelled rockets of the Minuteman and Polaris type will have become operational, general staffs will have a tendency to want to keep rockets of this kind continuously moving along the railroad tracks of the countries whose territories will be made available to them.

The invulnerability of a mobile rocket remains considerable only if it can be kept moving over vast spaces, thus making it highly difficult for the enemy to pinpoint its position at any given moment. The moment this space is restricted the entire area becomes an interesting priority target.

For that reason the people of Western Europe with their restricted territories have a vested interest in not welcoming visits from such dangerous guests and in seeing them banned forever from the regions they inhabit.

The ruling circles of most of the countries of Western Europe, on the other hand, are still far from realizing the benefits to be derived by their peoples from becoming part of a zone of "reduced armaments." If some of them fear and resent the presence on their territories of American strategic weapons, it is only to the extent to which they themselves are not in control and there is a growing tendency toward the setting up of autonomous national atomic striking power.

For a number of years now Great Britain has had its own national nuclear striking power. France counts on having such forces in the near future.

To justify the creation of French atomic striking forces General de Gaulle declared at a press conference on November 10, 1959:

> Who can say whether in the future, the political background having changed completely—that is something that has already happened on earth—the two powers having the nuclear monopoly will not agree to divide the world?

> Who can say that if the occasion arises the two, while each deciding not to launch its missiles at the main enemy so that it should itself be spared, will not crush the others? It is possible to imagine that on some awful day Western Europe might be wiped out from Moscow and Central Europe from Washington. And who can even say that the two rivals, after I know not what political and social upheaval, will not unite?

We hardly think that the fact that a West European country possesses a national atomic striking force is likely to permit it to engage in independent nuclear policy. Every holder of an atomic striking force is a potential aggressor and as such, rather than constitute a threat to either of the nuclear giants, is instead in need of protection from one of them.

Nor do we feel that the possession of independent atomic striking forces by the countries of Western or Central Europe could reduce Europe's chances of annihilation in the case of war between the nuclear giants. We feel on the contrary that it is likely to increase these chances enormously. No matter what efforts Great Britain, France and the other European countries may make in the field of nuclear armaments, the striking power these countries will be able to amass will always equal only a fraction of that of the two nuclear giants. It is conceivable that the striking power of some European country might have a deterrent effect when it is allied to one of the giants. But as an independent force it is more likely to act as a provocation than a deterrent. A striking force can only act as a deterrent if it is sufficiently great and sufficiently dispersed to be in a position to strike second. The potential for development of the striking forces of the countries of Western Europe and the size of their territories excludes this hypothesis.

If the contingency projected by General de Gaulle were to arise and Europe were really one day annihilated by American and Russian projectiles, this would undoubtedly happen because the two opponents would be trying to destroy the means of massive destruction situated in the middle area. The fact that these devices belonged to a European power and not to either of the two giants would hardly make the target less attractive, especially if the European government in question had no long-established and well-proven policy of neutrality. But then most of the advocates of the concept of an independent striking force fail to see it as a means for making possible the pursuit of a neutralist policy. Many on the contrary see in an independent striking force the necessary detonator for the vast striking force of the Alliance, that is to say, of the United States.

Professor P.M.S. Blackett writes in this connection in the *New Statesman* of December 5, 1959:

> In the dream world of some present-day military theorists the argument goes somewhat as follows. The value to Britain of an independent atomic capability is that it could be used to trigger off the American Strategic Air Command if a crisis arose in which the President would not order it into action unless his hand was forced. For instance, if Soviet radar picked up a missile traveling from Britain, the USSR would assume that a general attack had begun and retaliate against the whole Western system —or America would assume that they might assume this and immediately join in. So the British H-bomb was held to have a catalytic function in the sense that it gives Britain a share in the physical control of the SAC far more convincing than any formal agreement with the U.S.

Professor Blackett indicates the reasons why in his view a multiplicity of independent striking forces within the same alliance is deadly:

> . . . there cannot be the slightest doubt that if any medium rank power initiated atomic warfare with the intention of involving a great power, the inevitable reaction of the latter would be to disclaim immediately all responsibility and to state emphatically by all available means that it was taking no part. . . .

> There can be little doubt that if nuclear weapons do come into the sole possession of many NATO powers, either by independent manufacture or by gifts from the giant powers, then a common defense policy for Western Europe will become very difficult and NATO may tend to break up into a number of nuclearly armed and mutually suspicious states: in fact, possibly more suspicious of each other than of the USSR.

Thus, independent striking forces by their very nature tend to weaken the alliance they have made necessary.

For some time now there has been considerable talk about the creation of a "European" striking force. This is what Professor Blackett writes on the subject:

> In my view this situation cannot be altered by the building up of the much-discussed European as opposed to NATO deterrent—meaning by this a strategic and tactical nuclear capability under exclusive European control. I have failed to envisage any possible way in which a dozen independent nations could make arrangements for the joint control of such nuclear forces, which avoided on the one hand the danger of such divided and ponderous control as to remove its military value, and on the other, the much greater danger of careless or irresponsible action by one nation involving the others.

> In fact, I can see no plausible way in which the European defense community can survive either with its own jointly owned nuclear forces or with individual national nuclear forces. I feel that the present situation, with an American safety catch on all its own nuclear weapons, wherever situated, is much more stable than either of the above alternatives. . . .

The concept of a pan-European striking force is to be rejected for the very same reasons as those advanced earlier against the concept of national striking forces. The territory of Western Europe is too small and densely populated to permit such a force to have a deterrent effect.

The smaller European countries have particularly valid reasons for rejecting the entire concept. For if before it could be used this force had to rely on a system of consultation in which their agreement was indispensable, it would have no military value; and if the contrary were true, the small countries would almost automatically be marked for death and destruction.

It is to be hoped that very soon, before it is too late, the Europeans will grasp the idea that their best chance to escape annihilation is to be included in a reduced armament zone where they will remain outside the field of action of the much publicized "pre-emptive" blows and other action aimed against regions containing strategic bases.

The governments of the countries that are no nuclear giants are faced with the twin tasks of doing everything possible to render conflict between the two big powers improbable and offering the peoples of their own nations a chance to escape disaster should it unhappily come to pass.

We feel the governments of Western Europe could best fulfill this double task by advocating as a first step toward general and controlled disarmament the creation in Europe of reduced armament zones from which at least the carriers capable of transporting long-range massive destruction devices would be excluded.

One of the most disturbing aspects of the present period is the apparent lack of appreciation by governments of the most elementary interests of the populations of Western Europe. This is all the more remarkable since this attitude is much less pronounced in the United States, where important political figures have gone on record in favor of creating demilitarized zones and where as important an authority on matters of strategy as Dr. Bernard Brodie writes in his book, *Strategy in the Missile Age*, on the subject of the installation of IRBM rocket emplacements in Europe:

> Ideas about giving them protection by moving them about on the highway network of Europe overlook the security prob-

lem within those confined areas, the oppressiveness of such a spectacle to the peoples of western Europe and the fact that in any above-ground positioning these missiles can be destroyed by nuclear weapons exploding at distances of several miles. The enemy, in other words, would have to know only their approximate location, which his intelligence network operating in what is presumably peacetime could easily deliver to him.

For a number of political, psychological and technical reasons total disarmament does not seem feasible in the near future. But it is becoming more and more urgent to struggle against the ever greater and more imminent danger of possible surprise attack by engines of mass destruction against the adversaries' strategic bases. This danger is now very real and, as Dr. Brodie has written:

> So long as there is a great advantage in striking first, and under existing conditions the advantage would be tremendous, we must realize that even rational men could start a total war, and irrational ones would need no such justification.

The most effective way to lessen the probability of surprise attack would be to lessen the reasons which might lead either side to want to be the first to strike.

In a situation depending upon balance of terror both sides find themselves in permanent danger of being mutually destroyed. If the situation is to remain unchanged, then in order to continue with a certain degree of stability two essential conditions must be met:

1) Neither of the adversaries must believe he is in a posi-position to put the other *hors de combat* without the other having time to retaliate.

2) Neither must at any time believe himself to be in *imminent* danger of being hit before having time to retaliate.

For the first of these conditions to be met the strategic forces of both sides must possess a high degree of invulnerability. For the second, the warning period time preceding attack must not fall below a certain minimum indispensable for interpreting correctly the informational data indicating the existence of attack.

Great efforts have been made to meet the first of these conditions. In order to increase the invulnerability of the deterrent complex, both sides have resorted to increasing the number of their bases, to hardening them and achieving greater mobility and dispersal of armaments.

But let us make note of the fact that the methods chosen for increasing invulnerability have been chiefly those which simultaneously serve counterforce strategy. Relatively little has been done in the field of hardening bases, even though this method is at once more economical and less provocative.

Great effort is also being exerted to meet the second condition: perfecting and developing radar stations, construction of satellites of the Midas and Samos type which are intended for detecting enemy projectiles at the instant of their launching. Nevertheless the most radical measure possible for fulfilling the second condition, namely the obvious one of increasing the distance between the adversaries' strategic bases, does not seem slated for consideration since it would meet opposition from partisans of the strategy of counterforce.

The strategy of deterrence is thus subordinated to that of counterforce and is only projected insofar as it does not interfere with the latter. This is a patently dangerous situation, for counterforce strategy is based on the principle of the pre-emptive blow, which is hard to distinguish from a first blow.

It is impossible to carry to the limit the power of counterforce without at the same time prejudicing the equilibrium of the balance of terror.

The two main enemies of this equilibrium are the vulnerability and the speed of strategic arms. This speed is a most important factor in the strategy of counterforce, a strategy which finds itself diametrically opposed to the policy of strengthening the stability of the balance of terror.

There are those who mistakenly believe that possession of a major or primary deterrent, one which is properly protected and boasts a high degree of invulnerability, makes it possible without inconvenience to then add a secondary one, more vulnerable to be sure but better adapted to the strategy of counterforce, and that such a secondary deterrent would be effectively protected by the primary one.

This is a serious error, especially in the case of secondary deterrents located in relative proximity to the adversary, where warning signal time threatens to fall below the minimum mentioned above.

Should the enemy believe that absolute interdependence existed between the secondary and the primary deterrents, realization of the first of the two conditions we have described would not be influenced by the addition of secondary deterrents. But realization of the second would. The degree of stability of the balance of terror would thus be seriously affected.

Nor is it at all certain that the enemy would be convinced regarding the absolute interdependence of the deterrents. The hue and cry around the possibilities of limited war is hardly something to help nurture such convictions.

In a letter to the *New Statesman* of July 2, 1960 Bertrand Russell makes the following observation on this subject:

> The Soviet government has announced that any satellite of the U.S. which permits U2 flights from its territory will be obliterated. The British government has said that it will not permit such flights from British territory, but American militarists are pretty certain soon to find something which the Russians will dislike as much as U2 flights. Russia may then destroy every human inhabitant of Britain within an hour or two. Although America, at present, states and sincerely believes that the obligations of NATO would be fulfilled in such a case, there is much reason to doubt whether they would be when it came to the point. We should be dead and nothing could be done for us, and the only effect of coming to the defence of our corpses would be to spread equal destruction throughout America and Russia, and almost equal destruction throughout the world. I think the Russians might well calculate that America would not think this worth while.

If governments continue to sacrifice stability of the balance of terror to increases in the efficiency of those potential pre-emptive blows of which their military dream, the fate of humanity will soon be sealed. Again to quote Bernard Brodie:

> Technological progress could, however, push us rapidly towards a position of almost intolerable mutual menace. Unless something is done politically to alter the environment, each side before many years will have thousands of missiles accurately pointed at targets in the other's territory ready to be fired at a moment's notice.

Examining the conditions under which strategic arms would be called into action the same author writes:

> If a reaction system is to be sensitive enough to be promptly and reliably triggered when the real attack comes, it has to be sensitive enough to respond also to occasional false alarms. . . . There is always the danger, too, of an action which is provocatory to the similarly fidgety opponent. The real attack will come only once, if it comes at all, and the problem of maintaining a fine balance between alertness and calm will, if we are lucky, prevail over many years. The permitted reaction time is meanwhile rapidly becoming less, and the long-range ballistic missiles promise to reduce it to a hard minimum so short as probably to allow no time for counteractions that are not largely automatic.

and he adds:

> It is even possible that we shall build so much automaticity and sensitivity into our retaliatory response that it could be triggered by an "indication of hostile intent" rather than a hostile act. Such a development would probably be attributable more to absent-mindedness on the part of our political leaders than to design. . . .

General P. Gallois on the other hand sees in the automatic retaliatory blow a factor which, by making war independent of politics, would tend to increase deterrence. He writes in his book, *Strategy in the Nuclear Age:*

> An added paradox of this age is that we see Western democracies basing their security on a policy which would become

110

more or less meaningless if it were made to depend on popular consent. By way of consolation let us say that it is a question rather of something like a clock mechanism which the governments wind and rewind with the support of popular opinion, but whose actual motion like that of time eludes intervention.

It is high time that the attention of governments cease to be absorbed with questions of secondary importance and that they apply themselves instead to better understanding the significance of the mechanisms which have been set up by the military with such admirable professional zeal but, unfortunately, without regard for probable consequences.

Governments must without delay begin to address themselves to the task of dismantling those mechanisms whose eventual goals are becoming more and more obvious.

In line with this it would seem that the most urgent task is to prevent the strategic arms of presumptive adversaries from finding themselves at a weak distance from one another. To this end the disarmament of certain geographic zones is indicated, at least in regard to strategic arms. It does not seem futile to hope that the adversaries may agree under conditions of reciprocity to sacrifice a little of their power of counterforce in favor of maintaining stability of the balance of terror.

In order for it to be possible to achieve total or even partial controlled disarmament of certain geographical zones, it is essential to create as soon as possible within the United Nations the framework of the international control agency we spoke of earlier.

In order to achieve this first step it might be well to follow the lead of what has been accomplished in relation to nuclear explosion tests. The slow but positive progress of negotiations to discontinue these tests may be attributed to the fact that the negotiations themselves were preceded by a technical conference which defined the controls that would be necessary, thus providing a concrete base for the political negotiations.

We must hope that under the aegis of the United Nations a technical conference will be called in the very near future, charged with determining the terms of control needed to guarantee that certain geographical zones positively not serve as bases for surprise attack conducted with weapons of massive destruction, and also stating the lines along which it would be practical to set up the international body itself.

There is yet another facet of this subject that surely cannot fail to surprise the historians of the future, granted there are to be any; namely, that it should have been a continent uninhabited by human beings which man-made governments chose to save from the follies of war.

We welcome the recent treaty on the demilitarization of Antarctica as a very important positive fact and we trust the day will come when governments will want to extend to large sections of mankind the privileged system now reserved for penguins and seals. As we await the dawning of that day we at least hope that in case of conflict, always provided the bombs used are relatively "clean" and not too numerous, penguins and seals will survive and repopulate the earth.

BIBLIOGRAPHY

Antoine Allard, *Ferveur*. 38 Avenue E. Duray, Brussels.

General Sir Ronald Adam and Charles Judd. *Assault at Arms*. London: Weidenfeld and Nicolson, 1959.

Jacques Bloch-Morhange. *La stratégie des fusées*. Paris: Plon, 1958.

Bernard Brodie. *Strategy in the Missile Age*. Princeton University Press, 1959.

Alastair Buchan. *NATO in the 1960's*. London: Weidenfeld and Nicolson, 1960.

E. N. Dzelepy. *Désatomiser l'Europe? La vérité sur le Plan Rapacki*. Brussels: Editions Politiques, 1958.

Général P. Gallois. *Stratégie de l'âge nucléaire*. Paris: Calmann-Lévy.

Raymond L. Garthoff. *Soviet Strategy in the Nuclear Age*. New York: Frederick A. Praeger, Inc., 1958.

James M. Gavin. *War and Peace in the Space Age*. New York: Harper & Brothers, 1958.

Fernand Gigon. *Formula for Death: $E = mc^2$*, trans., Constantine Fitz-Gibbon. New York: Roy Publishers, 1958.

Victor Gollancz. *Devil's Repertoire; or, Nuclear Bombing and the Life of Man*. New York: Doubleday & Co., Inc., 1959.

H. W. Heckstall-Smith. *Atomic Radiation Dangers and What They Mean to You*. London: J. M. Dent & Sons, 1958.

Kenneth Heuer. *The Next Fifty Billion Years*. New York: Viking Press, 1957.

Robert Jungk. *Brighter Than a Thousand Suns*. London: Victor Gollancz and Hart Davies, 1958.

George F. Kennan. *Russia, the Atom and the West*. New York: Harper & Brothers, 1958.

Stephen King-Hall. *Defense in the Nuclear Age*. London: Victor Gollancz, Ltd., 1958.

113

Henry A. Kissinger. *Nuclear Weapons and Foreign Policy*. New York: Harper & Brothers, 1957.

Jules Moch. *Human Folly: To Disarm or Perish?* trans., Edward Hyams. London: Victor Gollancz, Ltd., 1958.

Jules Moch. *En retard d'une paix*. Paris: Ernest Laffont, 1958.

Philip John Noel-Baker. *The Arms Race: A Programme for World Disarmament*. London: Stevens & Sons, 1958.

Nuclear Explosions and Their Effects. Published by the Ministry of Information and Broadcasting, Government of India. Delhi: 1956.

Linus Pauling. *No More War*. New York: Dodd, Mead & Co., 1958.

Antoinette Pirie. *Fall Out; Radiation Hazards from Nuclear Explosions*. New York: John de Graff, Inc., 1959.

Bertrand Russell. *Power*. London: George Allen & Unwin, Ltd.

Bertrand Russell. *Common Sense and Nuclear Warfare*. New York: Simon & Schuster, Inc., 1959.

Bertrand Russell. *Portraits from Memory*. New York: Simon & Schuster, Inc., 1956.

Albert Schweitzer. *Peace or Atomic War?* New York: Henry Holt & Co., Inc., 1958.

Survival, a periodical published by Institute for Strategic Studies, 18 Adam St., London, W. C. 2.

Edward Teller and Albert L. Latter. *Our Nuclear Future: Facts, Dangers and Opportunities*. New York: Criterion Press, Inc., 1958.

Philip Toynbee. *The Fearful Choice: A Debate on Nuclear Policy*. Detroit: Wayne State University Press, 1959.

Wayland Young. *Strategy for Survival*. London: Penguin Books, 1959.